BACKSTAGE

NASHVILLE

D0562836

THE UNDISCLOSED STORY OF A
MAJOR LABEL RECORDING ARTIST

Wayne Warner

Backstage Nashville: The Undisclosed Story of a Major Label Recording Artist
© Wayne Warner 2019

ISBN: 978-1-925935-16-5 (Paperback)
        978-1-925935-17-2 (eBook)

A catalogue record for this book is available from the National Library of Australia

Lead Editor: Kristy Hoffman
Editor: Peta Culverhouse
Cover Design: Ocean Reeve Publishing
Design and Typeset: Ocean Reeve Publishing

Published by Wayne Warner and Ocean Reeve Publishing

Printed in America by Ocean Reeve Publishing
www.oceanreeve.com

Contents

Backstage Nashville

The Undisclosed Story of A Major Label Recording Artist

The fact that the amazing you is even holding this book in your hands is astounding to me. You hold also, my sincerest gratitude. Even more astonishing to me, is that the following pages exist to be read.

Albert Einstein wrote; "I do, in fact, believe that it is a good thing to show those who are striving alongside of us, how one's own striving and searching appears to one in retrospect." It is my attempt to do just that in the following pages, with respect to a music business that has been kind to my life, while at the same time, guarding the integrity of confidences entrusted to me.

While many aspects of our lives are different, in so many ways, we are all; "different the same", and share a common theme of ups and downs, celebrations and struggles. I hope that through this book, we both continue to gain an understanding that you and I … are not alone.

I confess that the crafting of this book was initiated with some contention on my part, and it gets a bit 'rank.' There are elements within the pages that depict situations for which I was told that if I didn't write, someone else would. As such, I wanted them to be expressed from my point of view, and as best as my memory would serve. I also committed that if it was to be written, I would dive into some areas of my life that I seldom do. I wanted to take the opportunity to connect with even one soul if such a personal expression would allow…

Working within the limitations of written language, I want to express my sincere thanks and gratitude to so many hearts and souls for contributing to the pages of my life; for imprinting every word connected to love and support within the binders of my journey.

To every radio station that ever spun a Wayne Warner song and welcomed me in to your studios.

To every soul who bought a ticket to the few shows I ever agreed to do. For me, you were the best part of the show.

To the B-Venturous Records Team.

To the Warner's Dance Hall crowd for a lifetime of good-time Saturday Nights.

To my mom and dad for being a mom and dad

To every musician who ever played on a Wayne Warner record, performed with me on stage, or inspired me from one.

To Calvin, Danny, Ryah, Kore, Al, Effie, Bob, Sarah, Pete, Scott Boskind, Ray Perkins and Mary Lou for their encouragement and support.

To Sis – for STILL being the canvas.

For – Kyle and Keenan

www.waynewarner.com
www.facebook.com/waynewarnermusic/
@turbotwangwayne

Chapter 1

Studio Discoveries

"By the grace of God
I was born and raised
In ordinary, small town USA
Kiss'n in the moonlight' a partying gang
It ain't hillbilly, its Turbo Twang."

— *TURBO TWANG*, WAYNE WARNER

I hate video shoots; the lights; the cameras; the gadgets, all with so many people behind them—none of whom I had ever met. Sandy, the one standing beside my tall stool in the make-up room, knew her stuff and was obviously accustomed to the chaos of soundstages. She pulled out her brushes, hair sprays, and utensils, like Marshall Dillon drawing a gun. While I have long been uncomfortable with being touched, I had grown accustomed to the "pretty people" side of the gig, and this made poor Sandy's work a challenge and, no doubt, her day's salary insufficient—at least, for now.

Even though the upcoming August fall season was starting to cool the Nashville Tennessee nights, the hot Southern sun baked my tour bus as the long day was about to begin. The huge soundstage was set for the song *Turbo Twang*, a song that was doing well for me on radio and—oddly enough—a country dance club smash. Dances were created for the song from all corners of the world and the "twangers" would stomp this tune right up the dance club charts. As far as the expansion of my fan-base goes, it was the song that had achieved the most for me. As an artist and a writer, it was one that I liked—the least. It was written as a kind of a sarcastic throw-back to a critic who had penned about my music in some magazine and didn't know how to "label" me. While he wrote a good critique, he ended up defining my sound as "Turbo Twang." I remember being at my home twenty-four hours of interstate north of the famous city in small-town Vermont at the time, and on one of my nightly walks around the block, the song was born. I played the song for my sister, confidante, and manager, Juanita Lee, who loved it. I, however, as a writer, liked songs with substance—songs you had to sharpen your pencil for—and I had no intentions of the song ever being heard. Several months later, after a Nashville recording session, I thanked the super talented cast of musicians that I often use on my records and stepped outside of the studio, taking in the city skyline at night while I sucked down a fix for my tobacco habit. When I re-entered the control room, I was tired and glad to be done for the day, but there was *that* song, coming out of the studio monitors. Sis had the band working up *Turbo Twang and* guided me to the vocal booth. The pickers, directed by session leader and co-producer, Troy Lancaster, caught the groove and got the party on tape. Even so, I was less than thrilled, but laid down one quick vocal, still planning to shelve the song. Label Partner, cousin, and financial guru, Ray Pronto, slipped the un-mastered and quickly mixed demo to his local radio station program director, Frank Bell. Frank was the program director for Froggy 104.3 on the outskirts of Pittsburgh, Pennsylvania. Among the original of our thirteen founding states and sitting in the northeastern and Mid-Atlantic region. The city is one of the state's major metropolitans. To me, Frank is one of the most genuine, classiest and kind men I have ever known in the business. The song hit the airwaves in megawatts and became an instant hit on the station. So much so, that we had to remove the *Turbo Twang* logo from the tour bus, as we would always get mobbed en route from Vermont to Nashville. It was my idea to invite Frank to have a starring role in the video, as he was one of the key players in the success of the song. Next to me on one of those high stools in the room of mirrors, sat Frank Bell in another make-up chair.

As Sandy plucked and applied, straightened, and sprayed, we passed the time talking about a visit that Ray, Juanita, Frank and I had made the day before, to a home on the outskirts of Music City. Family friends of Frank from the old Burgh neighborhood—Scott and Andrea—had just moved to town from the Pittsburgh area, along with their thirteen-year-old son, Austin, and his older sister. The move was made so their young daughter could be near the music scene to hook her young fifteen-year-old teenage dreams of fame upon a star.

Because the family was friends of Frank's, from the ole Burgh neighborhood and the young lass was a fan of *Turbo Twang*, our video crew accepted the invite to their home for dinner. Oddly enough, as we entered the sprawling home, good ol*e Turbo Twang* was playing throughout the property, via the elaborate central stereo system. Scott and Andrea were amazing hosts, and talk flowed easily. Their young daughter—tall for her age and golden blonde—had a personality that wore the room. Small talk turned to discussing the music business, and the Music Row connections that we might be able to engage for the young singer. She lit up when talk turned to music, and it wasn't long before her guitar case was empty on the floor and the jamming began. She glowed as we tossed songs back and forth from our flat top guitars on the family couch, and her talent was immediate and undeniable. Frank, Ray, Sis, and I were all captivated by her professionalism and stunned by her delivery and her all-around "star power" for someone of such a young age. We all knew that she had the "it factor" the minute she opened her mouth and strummed her six strings. No one knows what "it" really is, but she had "it" in bold, red, capital letters! Little brother, Austin, was reserved and polite but reminded me of, well, me, in that he preferred to be in the background. Juanita and I were both astonished by how his older sister loved and doted on him. Ray and Scott, both cut from a businessman cloth, busied themselves with businessman talk and Andrea, Juanita, the "star gazer," and I talked songs and stages.

While Andrea busied herself in the kitchen, Austin and his older sister gave us a tour of the house. I remember little of it, but Juanita, always into décor, was captivated by the design of the place and the teenage singer's recording studio set-up. Juanita also remembers vividly that the jam session had moved outside to the picnic table, and the music played on. My memory is vague about the whole scene, but I do recall that we mentioned a co-write. The young singer threw out some lines and a title that she had seemingly tossed out on the spur of the moment. Even at such a young age, I was struck by her ability to paint a picture with lyrics and I grabbed my ever-ready cassette recorder from my guitar case, to capture our thoughts. Her title, *The Middle of The Light*, I think, may have been born from our discussion about my video shoot the following day, and my dislike for them, and being in the spotlight. She wanted it all more than anything. The direction of the song, as she took it, was a love story to someone – or to God – and I loved the idea. We captured a lot of it and talked about finishing it up at some point at a later date.

Other than the impact of her talent, the impromptu writing session was what I considered the most uneventful aspect of the day; we were just a couple of singers throwing down a few lines. As Sis recalls it, with the song on tape, we jammed on until Andrea rang the dinner bell, following up with more great conversation and new friends made. An impending early morning wake-up call to shoot the dreaded video would dictate our early evening exit, and Frank, Ray, Sis and I said, "Thank you and good night" to Scott, Andrea, young Austin, and Taylor Swift.

The video shoot went as video shoots go, with cameras so close to my face I thought they were checking for cavities. They would play the track and I would do my best to move my thick lips in time to the way I sang it on the record. Over and over. Watching the great dancers the video producers had brought in was fun, and I celebrated their talent and ability to quickly learn new moves and marks, but, the highlight for me was Frank Bell's acting ability. He was amazing: an absolute pro from the second the cameras rolled, especially for a guy who spent much of his career unseen behind a mic at radio a station. He really did steal the show, and I was happy to have him.

The day was busied with Frank and me visiting and revisiting the makeup room. In there, the talk between us, as well as with Sis and Ray, was very much about our visit with Taylor the day before and strategizing about how we were going to help her get through the tightly closed doors of the business. We did find it fascinating how much Sandy, the make-up lady, was attracted to our dialogue about the young singer.

Finally, after a long day, the director called it a wrap. I was relieved and ready to pack and get on my tour bus waiting in the parking lot. In it, I knew was my favorite pair of sweats: the ones with all the holes in them. The ones that I had spent years to make fit just right, and that everyone kept threatening to throw away. We gathered our belongings, thanked the film crew, and Sandy Borchetta packed up her make-up case. No one knew that the musical landscape ... was about to change.

Chapter 2

Stage One

"Play an old song, would you play one for me
One from the way, things used to be
Play an old song, and take me away
Take me back with a song, from yesterday."

– *Song From Yesterday*, Wayne Warner

It was around 1968, and my uncle's voice hollered, 'It's square dance time,' as he did every Saturday night at Buzzy's Barn Dance, up in the far northern corner of Vermont. My home state is the second smallest by population in our good ole USA, and I grew up about as far northeast as you can get to the Canadian border while still being red, white and blue. Big letters on the side of the white home for cows said, "North Hill Barn," but everyone called it Buzzy's after the friendly guy who owned it, and Buzzy would take your three dollars as you entered the loft. The Warner Band had the regular Saturday night gig and, for me, the sawdust on the dance floor was like gold dust on the walkway to the gates of Heaven. The song hits of the day by Charlie Pride, Loretta Lynn, and Johnny Cash would echo out of the old Traynor speakers, and I would sit on the edge of the stage and watch my dad and his band in awe as it all came to life. The band played the songs, set the pace, the mood, and the atmosphere, and the crowd would respond at their command. My dad had been the leader of the family band for years, and he was even beckoned from the stage six years earlier, on May 4 1962, when my mom went into labor with her second born. I had been at my dad's feet whenever the music was played ever since. Now, while us three kids hung by the stage, my mom worked in the little kitchen selling sodas and steamed hot dogs. I would sit and regard with great reverence how my dad's carpenter-callused hands could glide so smoothly along the frets of his Gibson mandolin or flat top guitar. I know now that with each pick of my dad's strings, the turbo twang sound that the famous critic attached to me was being planted and would influence my musical compositions, no matter what genre I explored.

I grew up in a middle-class family in the very rural Vermont town. My dad worked hard, and my mom made the new house that dad had built, a home. I was the middle and admittedly awkward child, but tried my best to fit in with older sis Juanita, and younger brother, Allan. The three of us, all two years apart, grew up knowing everyone in the small, one-paved-highway town.

Besides being a carpenter, my dad was licensed to work on Motorola televisions. Having to clear one of those big ole deep-boxed television sets off the kitchen table for supper time was a common scene in the Warner household. I can still smell the scent of freshly soldered wires blending with the aroma of spaghetti sauce.

Traveling was something we did often as a family back then. With the small camper hitched to the Studebaker station wagon, off we would go to one of dad's destinations. These long trips became routine to us kids, and as the mile markers passed, dad would play those eight-tracks of Merle, Johnny, Porter, Buck, and Charlie, or Mom would try to tune in to a country radio station for more hits of the day. Little bro Allan, not the music lover of the bunch, would often complain about the "noise" he had to endure in the back seat, as Juanita and I were singing along; song after song. After many miles of me pounding out the drum beats on the back of Dad's seat, we would finally be told that the show was over. Allan had won some peace, for about as long as it would take for the carburetor to burn through at least a gallon's worth of gasoline.

Back on the home front, my dad's band practices were a regular event in our living room, and Mom would have sandwiches at the ready. At some point, I was given a wooden toy guitar of my very own. Although it barely made a sound, I did have a few chords down that my dad's brother, Uncle Alden and Dad had taught me, and during those rehearsals in our living room next to our own Motorola, I was part of the Warner Band. I lived for those Saturday nights at Buzzy's. Little did I ever dream then—or perhaps I did—that my leader-of-the-band, Dad would someday be the relief driver of my *Turbo Twang* tour bus.

Chapter 3

Parking lots

And so it was in 2005, I was sitting at my table on the bus outside our West End Nashville suites. The place had become a second home to Sis and me, and the hotel staff were our Music City family. The two of us were in Nashville a lot for meetings with management and publicists, as well as radio interviews and recording sessions. The fact that I would never move out of Vermont would demand several trips, but I was willing to make the trade. 16th Avenue, Nashville, Tennessee, had become a major destination of dreams. On the outskirts of the city, this little series of one-way streets generate much of what reaches the ears for the masses created by the genre. While modern structures dot the old streets, the heartbeat of mother country music still has a strong pulse in small historical non-descript frames. Many songs were written and recorded by dreamers who had walked in with nothing and left with gold records. Even more, exited the famous Music Row with less than what they came with. I had seen what the Row had done to too many of my peers when they become absorbed in the chaos of chasing chart positions and the celebrity of it all. I loved to go to Nashville, fill my emotional cupboards with enthusiasm, kinship, and creativity, then return home, and pig out on the whole of it. I failed miserably at it, but as an artist, I was determined at least to try not to become ... what I do.

While the accommodations at our usual hotel hang' were great, the table in the galley of the bus was where I liked my coffee the most. The 45-foot decked-out Prevost was where we always found ourselves, as it housed all our belongings and allowed quick access to our working needs. I would usually enter the hotels on the road only for the use of the treadmills; the staff would always open the rooms to the gym for me after the usual hours. It really did seem strange to me how differently you were treated if you were delivered on a massive tour bus and your face recognized as the same one that graced local posters. However, I appreciated the gesture without complaint.

The scenery outside the bus windows at our Nashville base was a familiar one whenever we were there. We shared the huge but somewhat hidden parking section of the hotel with two other tour buses, whose riders often seemed to have the same schedule as ours. And as always, there they were.

One stood out among all the grand tour buses that mine had ever shared pavement with. Airbrushed on each of the sprawling sides was a masterpiece of a sunset with a lone Indian on a horse. While I know him only in passing, it seems that he too liked his coffee on his bus, and I would say hello to Willie Nelson on many mornings as we both sat side by side, each in our own quiet abodes, sucking down caffeine. However, he always came off his bus in much better spirits than I. Just sayin'.

The other bus in the lot was no slouch either. Glossy black with brightly colored and well-placed stripes, it was there almost every time we were. Those of us inside the business knew why it was in town a lot in those days. I knew the guy the bus carried also only in passing, and his life and mine had some unique music industry connections that would have a huge impact on both of our lives. I liked his music alright, but I was a fan especially for his reputation for taking no bull from the powers-that-be in our shared profession. One that holds more than its fair share of the monopolies that inhabit all forms of the entertainment field. He pushed back and not only relative to the business side, he would also sing his views, both personal and political, in his manly falsetto, right to the top of the album sales charts. Such was a rarity around these bright lights and he usually seemed to come out on top.

The guy on the big, black bus had a small vanity plate on the back that said "Big Dog" and had a smash hit that served as a number one middle finger to his former record label, who had told him that his career was pretty much over. The song, *How Do You Like Me Now* was a huge hit and would help to let his former label know … that Toby Keith was far from over.

The reason for Toby's frequency in town was that he and a former major label player were partnering to form their own independent label. Toby had been pushed around enough. Borrowing from his vanity plate, the new enterprise was to be called Show Dog Nashville, with Toby as the flagship artist. Toby had chosen his partner well, and the guy knew how to make a hit out of a record. On that there is no doubt. Their goal was to be an independent player that would rival the majors. Toby had the clout and his partner had the knowledge and the connections. All seemed a go and the Music Row presses spared no ink in spreading the buzz. Toby would soon begin work on a new album for his own label, and his partner would start the task of looking for new, young, and exciting acts to sign to the new operation. His name was Scott Borchetta, and while all of this was taking place, another Borchetta was powdering the shine off my nose and paying close attention to our talk about a new young gal in town on the set of *Turbo Twang*—that would be Sandy, aka Mrs. Scott Borchetta and things were about to happen.

Chapter 4

Molded

You could hear the school bell ring from my house. It was halfway around the square block and the school building was a simple, tall, white rectangle. Its job was to aid with the education of the town's kids; grades one through eight. With two grades and one teacher per classroom, it would average around fifteen to twenty young minds in front of the long, wall chalkboard.

Miss Pudvah's challenge was to ready all those in her classroom to move next door into the third and fourth-grade class at the end of the school year. Now, I'm sure there had been occasions in the old teacher's life that had forced a smile to her lips, but I never saw it, and I was scared to death of the woman. To me, there really should be some kind of law that says when your bellybutton's in your cleavage, it's time to retire. But ole lady Pudvah wasn't my only nemesis.

Even in first grade, school was a tortured existence for me. Bullying was a term that was not yet employed, but as scrawny as I was, when it came to torment, I was the wide receiver. Helping matters none was the fact that the Warner family was a close and expanded assembly, and as such, owned much of, or were involved in, a lot of the town's properties and what little politics there were. And for that, I was viewed as a stuck-up rich kid. In fact, I was neither. Yes, for the area, my family had done okay, but while I have learned to mask it when required, I was and remain extremely shy and uneasy around crowds of any kind. This made the bullseye even bigger.

By this time, I had my first real guitar, and getting home from school and hiding behind it was my sanctuary and my sanity. I remember well the day that my mom came to pick me up from school early because the guitar had arrived at the Sears and Roebuck catalogue store. At twenty miles and thirty minutes away, Newport was the nearest town for shopping, and the ride to pick up my prize seemed to last an eternity. But it was worth it. Stained with a starburst finish, this thing of beauty was to my young eyes a method of transport, an instrument of escape. It was almost like dads, and it was mine. It wasn't long before there was an eight-year-old boy, with messy hair and a few freckles around his nose, standing in the back of his dad's stage with that prize guitar, strumming a few chords to Johnny Cash's *A Ring of Fire* during those Saturday night gigs. I was nervous and shy but excited, and I would strum for all I was worth until my young eyelids grew weightier than my enthusiasm. Then it would be time to join my sister and brother on the floor next to the empty instrument cases. We would fall asleep to the rhythm until the last waltz was played and we were loaded into the car.

During the week, Mom always filled the house with the sounds of her vacuum cleaner and country music. She had a pile of country albums that she would load onto that old stereo and Conway or Porter would sing pretty for hours. Mom did love her Porter Wagoner. We also had AM radio with two choices for country music on the dial: WIKE in Newport, or we could tune in to Charlie Stone and Craig Ladd from WKDR, way out of Plattsburgh, New York.

Buzzy's Saturday night dances would offer a lot of grown-up insight to our young existence. No one in our immediate family had ever let alcohol or tobacco pass their lips, so the smoke-filled loft and the some-times-odd behaviors we would see became a part of our musical outing one night a week. Dad's three youngsters had become a fixture on the scene to the crowd, and under the watchful eyes of our parents, we were protected by them and pretty much all who had bought a ticket of admission.

During this time, an early Christmas morning found a full metallic-blue set of drums next to the tree with my name on them. At nine-years-old, my cousin and the full-time drummer in my dad's band broke his arm on the family farm. The next thing I knew, me and my dad were loading up my blue beauties and drumsticks. All those long family trips and keeping time with the old eight-track tapes by pounding on the back of my dad's driver's seat had paid off. It was Saturday night, and I had my first official job in the band. Uncle Alden on guitar to my right, Dad to my left, and Aunt Priscilla sang the lead on the female hits of the time. The five-day school weeks were hell, but on Saturday nights, I was kicking the beat and I was king. The family band played those Saturday night gigs while at the same time designing and erecting what would be destined to become the largest dance hall in the state of Vermont. My dad, grandfather, and uncles drove every nail in the place, and watching it come up from the ground was a sight to see, not only for the family, but for the community as well.

While Dad was building this vast structure, Mom, as always, kept the house and home a beautiful and warm place to grow up. While not a churchgoer, she wore her faith like a sweater by her actions and her tenderness. While not common, she would talk of God and asked that we would pray for this neighbor or that one when there was a concern. While I couldn't quote you a line of Ephesians or a verse from the book of James, a belief in something good was instilled in us and would often, usually during school recesses, be called upon to sustain me. Likewise, my dad usually distanced himself from talk of an organized religion, and no matter his degree of denial, lived a life that proved respect for a force of a higher plain.

I was eleven years old in May 1973, when Warner's Dance Hall had its grand opening. Its official name was the Missisquoi Manor—a tribute to the river that ran behind it and our house—but it was and will forever be known, as Warner's. By the time I was fourteen, I was off the drums and had become the cute little chubby-cheeked lead boy singer of the band. Having a younger element brought a new dynamic to the sound and one my dad would sometimes struggle with. Along with his Haggards and Jones' tunes, I was introducing songs like Bob Seger's *Old Time Rock and Roll* and Creedence's *Have You Ever Seen the Rain*. This was a whole new world for me. People were looking at me, but this time with acceptance, appreciation, and perhaps even a little adoration. The applause was exhilarating and such a contrast to my usual weekday existence. But, of course, there's always a trade-off, isn't there? No one else would ever know what women and men alike, fed on booze and atmosphere, liked to do to a cute little, chubby-cheeked fourteen-year-old lead boy singer in the band.

Chapter 5

Radio Rodeo

Radio had been kind to me and so was mother country music. We *Turbo Twang*-ed from one end of the country to the other and worked with some of the most famous names in the business. This wasn't my first rodeo with radio and even while I had a short stint on Atlantic Records, I had been rewarded kindly on the independent charts. I liked the word "independent" and what it stood for as far as the nature of a person goes. But sadly, in the music business, the title comes affixed with a stigma. That is to say, if you're an independent artist, the perception is often that you're not good enough to be deserving of the Golden Key that would get you on a major label. That analogy, of course, pegs into the bright red of the bullshit-o-meter. Many *choose* to avoid the politics and the mechanics of the majors where money—not music—is the bottom note, and the only one that matters, whether it's on key or not.

However, I do deem the stigma as somewhat deserving. Primarily for the fact that anyone who thinks they can sing, because they can bring moisture to Gramma's eye when they squeal out a note or two, while at the same time, has blood oozing from the ears of every poor canine within a four-mile radius, can also go out in the garage with a computer and make a record. And guess what? They lick a stamp and send these sum' bitches to the already overbooked deejays who get a ton of attempts at "independent" success every day. In the pile is perhaps the next superstar of the year, but who's going to go through the pile? So goes the problem and there comes the discredit of being an "independent." This is, of course, a huge benefit to the dominating and smirking majors and a sad state of affairs for the business as a whole. A business whose corporations will do all they can to keep even the most gifted and even *discovered* "indies" off their turf.

While I was working on the *Turbo Twang* album, big news was made by a friend of mine who, as an indie, would rattle the majors and assume one of their coveted chart positions with a song that many of you would know. A Billboard article wrote accurately that it "marked the first time in over 40 years a new artist, on an independent label, had obtained a top 10 hit." What it did NOT say was that it cost well over a million dollars to do so (If you see Mrs. Steven Rudy, tell her I said hello). I have sincere passion and concern for the new and struggling artists these days, but go for it anyway, have fun doing it, and take it all the way, baby. This cat's on your side, and so are many others.

I mentioned before in these ramblings, that I knew what would work for me, and more importantly, what would not. I knew that as far as singers go, I sure as hell was nothing special. What I attribute to any success that I had achieved was that I had developed a sound. This happened by my desire to *never* imitate another singer, even when doing their covers in the family band. This was by choice, but I confess to you freely that my lack of aptitude would also have inhibited me from doing so.

If there is one thing I do like about the song *Turbo Twang*, is that in it, I wrote a line that uses the phrase "where that Missisquoi River flowed." I had spent some time on the small riverbank behind my house, and I always found it intriguing that the only fish that were going along with the flow were eff'n dead.

That approach to making my records, combined with the support of my family, as well as the integrity they had instilled in me, paid off.

Pretty much friendless and sheltered growing up, I watched my family closely and observed that what they did, they did well and with honor. It was my desire to do music in the same fashion. I was very fortunate to connect with, befriend, and utilize some of the most famed and sought-after musicians and studios in Nashville. That combination, along with a large heaping of the faith my mama taught me, seemed to bring the right mix that many of the more adventurous radio deejays liked. I guess a few of them spent some time by a river or two themselves.

Despite the growing dimensions of controlled radio restrictions by the major players and mergers, there were, and are, many great people in radio who entered the forum for their love of music. These great people, along with their equally devoted listeners and fans had taken more than a few of my records to respectable charting positions and were much of the reason I spent many hours on my bus. As Juanita was head of the promo team, she had gotten to know many of these incredible people in radio via countless phone calls and radio seminars. Going to visit and personally meet them, do radio interviews, and hang-out on the bus with them, was always a great learning experience and an exhausting blast, while at the same time supporting a new record.

Sis and I would spend time between stops on the road with me doing some writing and calling home and her planning strategies, creating artwork for ads and keeping an eye on the status of promotions. We would also kill time with antics and a lot of conversation. While we were schooled on how to look the parts we played, our backwoods Vermont know-how sometimes failed us.

We would often laugh about the time when a few years earlier, my former co-manager Steve, a neighbor of Alan Jackson's, had invited us to his expansive home, for dinner in the high-brow part of town. Sis and I were comfortable with paper plates and disposable cups and knew we were in trouble the minute we walked in, and Steve's wife seemed disgusted by my jeans. Sis's black dress matched my shirt, but we were apparently underdressed for her liking. The long table was immaculate, with extensive, deep, hand-carvings from end to end. At each setting was silverware like we had never seen before and seemed to stretch for miles. For us, one fork would do. We looked at each other like, *Are you kidding me? What utensil are you supposed to use first?* – "where ta' hells the car keys? The silverware – the crystal and china, are you kidding me?"

When we sat at the massive spread, Sis said, "Just watch what they do," and the stare-down began. Turns out, the guests are supposed to begin first. This guy's wife was not too impressed with these northern hicks and couldn't wait to get us off her street, never mind out of her home. We couldn't wait either. Sis and I were starving but barely nibbled.

Finally, they brought out these white, powdered dessert ball contraptions and left them on the table for us, as they, to my mind, returned to the kitchen to plan their strategy to get us out of their house. In their absence, Sis and I dove onto the white powdered treats like gravity rode a downpour, and realized that our black clothes were covered in the stuff, and worse, we had filled the art carvings in the dark table with the sweet flakes. Panicking, we tried to dig the stuff out of the gaps with one of the thousands of silverware utensils at our disposal and wiping our clothes, but none of it was having a rapid effect.

It was Sis's idea to blow in the crevasses for all we were worth just as they re-entered the damn room. All the crystal in the room had lost its shine to be sure. When the sugar dust finally cleared, it was easy to identify that the high-class lady had no sense of low-class humor. Her eyes were the size of fifty cent pieces, and her eloquently manicured eyebrows had departed upwards, somewhere under her hairline. We thanked them for a great evening and bid them good night. In Alan Jackson's yard, we pulled the car over because we were laughing too hard to drive. We were never invited back!

Chapter 6

My First Recording

At my ripened age of fifteen, Warner's Dance Hall was booming. Located in the center of our little town, people would come from miles away for the big night out in the country. Educated by my dad, my Uncle Alden, and Aunt Priscilla, I had learned how to manage a crowd. By this time, Juanita had taken Aunt Priscilla's place as the lead female vocalist, and what a duo we made. How "Unc," as I always referred to Uncle Alden, and Dad were able to keep up with these younger singers and the newer demographic it brought in, still amazes me. Juanita and I worked off each other as if we were one body and the crowd reacted. I was always more about the song and the delivery. Sis was all performance. The combo, along with the band, brought an energy that resonated and connected with the Saturday night assembly. Warner's became the place to go and its 500-seat capacity was often overflowing.

The uniqueness of my local prominence from performing at Warner's made matters with school and my peers considerably worse. Being almost overwhelmingly embraced and accepted from my perch on the Saturday night stage, to a place of ridicule and rejection on Monday mornings was for me, an odd and almost impossible transition. I was alienated in all forums when it came to the school arena. There was no one saving a seat for me on the bus or at the lunchroom table.

Unlike the stage, where I was in the spotlight, in the classrooms and the hallways of school, I wanted to be totally invisible. If I heard laughter; I assumed it was directed at me. If there was name calling – I was sure they were talking to, or at – me. There was always the alienation and the high voltage declarations of "otherness". Mom and Dad tried to understand and be supportive, but the harassment and the degradation that came with the bullying, as well as my lack of understanding of it, would be something I would try to endure alone. I was always the last one "not to be picked" for teams. I would just be the one left standing there – left over after all the others were selected. Being a boy, and "big ones weren't supposed to cry," made wiping my tears as I walked down our short driveway to the bus, something I was even more ashamed of. But I did my best and would take the thirty-minute ride of eternity to Newport's North Country Union High.

I did have one friend there, among the large high school crowd. There was one face that was always happy and would continuously welcome me. My opposite in every respect; I was a rail and she wasn't. She wore big-framed, thick glasses and she was my pal. Cynthia D. was bullied worse than I, but seemed to have built up a resilience that I admired. It was a daily ritual that the same crew would bounce off her and toss the books out of her hands. I always thought, *Someday, somebody's gotta do something about that.* She would always manage to pull a smile, pick up her books, and go on her way. She may not have known it, nor perhaps did I at the time, but knowing she was there would get me through the days, somehow.

Luckily, Saturday would always come. On stage, with my guitar as my shield, I was in my zone. I always liked the floor monitors turned down so I could hear my voice slap back at me from the massive wall at the end of the huge dance floor. *Wow, was that me? Were all these people actually listening to me? Without laughing, and even clapping?* That was my voice! Who was this guy they liked so much, yet others so misunderstood? To these questions, I still search for answers.

When I would get off the school bus at the end of a long day, I would go to my room and head for my other friend: my Sears and Roebuck guitar. We spent a lot of time together and had even written a song or two. With a little ingenuity and two cassette recording decks, that guitar and I made our first recording; this was something I took to and felt comfortable doing.

Through that microphone and recorder, I could have a voice, share my thoughts, have opinions, and I knew this to be true, because I could hear it back through my headphones. This fish began to at least, tread its own waters and I knew what I wanted to do, or I was awakened to the realization that it was the only thing I could do.

There was only one recording studio in the entire state of Vermont, and I was surprised that we had even the one for such a rural area. Green Mountain Records, a three-hour drive away, was an eight-track studio with mattresses on the walls for soundproofing, but for me, the place was magic. The band had worked hard to rehearse two songs and at fifteen years old, while all my midweek in-school tormentors were honing their badgering tactics, I was behind a gigantic microphone about to make my first record. The experience was amazing, and when the red light came on, the band would play the intro and my hormonal changing voice would find the notes. This was big-time for this lost and confused kid, but on vinyl, a part of me at least had found a comfortable home.

One morning, the following week, and back in the long halls in the "hells of learning," I was once again greeted by my only buddy Cynthia D and her always ready smile. For me, the extended walls of the thin, grey school lockers set the tone for the color of my day, she was the only ray of sun, and once again, these same gents knocked the books from her arms folded at her chest. I thought; *This time, its time to change "somebody's" name to "me"*. I ignored their commands and picked up her books and handed them back to her. I don't remember feeling any pain, but I quickly understood that the blood on the floor was mine.

I said goodbye to Cynthia, threw my books in a large brown trash can on the way out the door on that, my last day of school. Mom and Dad were less than thrilled about my decision to quit school, but knew that I could take no more. A few days later, and by pure coincidence on my sixteenth birthday, I heard my voice, and my song, on the radio and that song, was about to take me on a journey that I could never have dreamed of.

Chapter 7

Stages

I always tried to make myself as comfortable as possible out there in my new universe. I was very blessed to have the family I had, and they were able to be not only a part of my team, but to me: THE team. Incorporated with my Nashville band was Unc, right there at my side and a reminder of all those Saturday nights at Buzzy's barn dance. Not only was he a part of the band, but he and his wife, Lisa, along with my dad were primary bus drivers and were able to get us wherever we were supposed to be on time. We became one out there, as an artist, as a label, as a band, as "easy-breezers" caught by a hurricane, always managing to find our way and land on our feet somewhere behind a microphone in our new land of chaos. It was a major and rapid lifestyle change for us, and together we kept each other grounded and in check. While stress was high and miles were many, disagreements were few and laughs were plenty. We also had Charlie, who had driven us for many miles, but we sometimes had to share him with other artists who had come to love him as we did.

It was one stage or radio station after another, and yet another a little farther on down the road. I would always try to forget where I was the night before so I wouldn't say how great it was to be in Fort Wayne, Indiana, when I was now in fact in Leesville, Louisiana.

We were on an especially long radio tour that would take us through Colorado, the Dakotas, and the south-western states. Due to the length of the run, our regular radio tour team made up of our dad, Unc, Charlie and Lisa couldn't go, and, our other standby driver was called out for a road run with one of his other regular clients, Whoopi Goldberg. Sis and I were sent a driver named Dave, who I swear should have come with a seeing-eye dog. If you wanna get on the right side of Jesus, let this guy haul your ass around the western mountainside ledges for a few weeks, and if you ain't praying to God then, you need some kind of exorcism, I'm here to tell you that right now.

One night, as the bus was rolling down the interstate and Sis was back in her bunk focused on the next day's agenda, I slapped a coffee in the microwave. At the days' end, and when the chaos quieted, the old Wayne would get restless and want to retreat to the sanctuary of home. But good ole driver Dave was chasing down those white lines and had the windshield pointing even farther away, and I was in it for the ride. So, like many times before, I grabbed my old cassette recorder from my guitar case to see what I had thrown down for song ideas. Sometimes, I would hear something that would inspire me, and the ink would flow from the pen to get me through another "somewhere" night. On the tapes, I would whisper lines that I thought might be good, song titles that I had come up with, or melodies I thought might be a hook. I pushed the play button and listened to a few ideas, made some notes, fast-forwarded, rewound, and then, there, what was that? Who was that? At first, I was confused by the sound of a female voice vibrating the little speaker of the machine. And then, I thought, *Wow.* It was the song that the teenage girl and I were working on back at her house and came up within two seconds! What was her name again? Oh yeah, Taylor. Taylor Swift. A few more listens to the spontaneous and off-the-cuff little co-write once again amplified her skill and reminded me of our commitment and desire to support her in any way we could. The writer's cap was on and no matter how many guardrails Dave might have taken out over the next few hours, I was in my zone. I wanted this song to be perfect for Taylor. She had introduced the title, a hook, and some great lines. Knowing she was a fan of *Turbo Twang,* I rocked it up a bit from her original slower feel and tried to rope it in. We all knew that she would be needing strong material to secure the right deal and I wrote, crossed out, rewrote, and made sure to keep it in the original direction that we had crafted so briefly that day at her house. Truckers passed, miles passed, and the candle burned out as driver Dave rolled on, talking on his phone to other drivers, both to stay awake and to pass the time. A few more edits to tie in with her melody on top of the chorus and the song *The Middle of The Light* was finished, and I couldn't wait for her to hear it.

I knew I had a busy radio day coming in a few hours. I thought about home and the distance I was from it both in miles and lifestyle. It's amazing how lost you can feel on a highway and not just geographically. The cassette recorder went back in the case and *The Middle of The Light* would, for the second time, be forgotten.

There were moments on the stage that were breathtaking. I would stare into the spotlight and get lost. The crowd and I were one, the band was on, and the sound system and lights were performing with me. On most of those nights, the many hours that I had been on stage with my dad befriended me, and I was able to sell the songs and really, what had become the act. But after the show, and during the long autograph and photo-op sessions, anxiety would drown out the surroundings and take control of my inner and center stage. I would always wonder why they would want a signature from me. Don't they know who I am? Don't they know that I'm the guy who was called names, spat on, ridiculed, and the last one "not to be picked" in gym class? Now, here I am, with security at my side and women wanting me to sign their breasts.

I loved the people, but as I signed those CDs, one after another, I found myself having a love/hate relationship for the guy gazing back at me from those plastic jewel cases. On the covers of my albums, I looked happy, content, and sure. But the guy signing the CDs was glad to sign "Best Wishes" in black, permanent marker right over the face of the guy in the picture. I did, however, love that people were there, that they appreciated my work. I was grateful and shook every hand I could. Meeting them one-on-one would get me through and down the road to do it all again.

One great solace was in fact, those people. The skylines changed, the alphabets of the radio station call letters altered, but the people were amazing wherever my boots came off the bus. For me and my somewhat isolated history, the fact that I had been invited into so many lives always amazed me. Music was powerful. Via three chords and three minutes, I had been a part of so many life events through digital format. My songs had been played at weddings, graduations, birthday parties, and funerals. I had been in their living rooms, in their cars, and on their television sets. The contrast between my old life of hidden tears and secret panic and the new life of crowds and autograph sessions was a collision. Great and unknowing people, both in my old and my new life, somehow kept me from becoming a complete and total wreck in the middle.

With a solid family structure, Ray's astounding business sense, and Sis's magnetic personality and ahead-of-the-curve approach, we had grown rapidly, perhaps at a pace that I was not able to comprehend. Like you, I had been molded by my youth. And, like us all, my mold too had its share of dents. While the make-up and the stage clothes did their external job, the inside was growing spiritually, emotionally, and physically ill. But for now, the show goes on. The show always goes on ... doesn't it?

Chapter 8

Nashville Calls

In 1978 and not long after my sixteenth birthday, and hearing my little song recorded with the family band on the radio, the phone rang. It was one of the old phones, the kind that hung on the wall with a cord attached that would allow you the total freedom of movement, for up to five feet.

Whether my ever-present mom was cooking or cleaning I'm not sure, but I was the one who answered the call. The caller asked with a southern drawl if this was the home of Wayne Warner, and I told him who I was. He asked if my father was at home. I tried to think if I had done anything wrong and thought it must be someone trying to get me back in school. Dad was at work, so I took his number and gave a promise of a return call.

Intrigued, later that night, Dad dialed the 615-area code and number to learn that it was a Nashville producer who had heard his son's record and wanted to produce a Nashville recording session. I mean, really? What? How?

It turns out that Charlie Stone, from that radio station we often listened to just across our Vermont border out of Plattsburgh New York, found something in my hormonal changing voice that he found fresh and unique. Unbeknown to us, he went through his radio station's stack of top artists of the day to find out who the mainstream producers were. He settled on the name Ray Pennington. Ray Pennington had been behind many hits at the time and had written and produced the hit *I'm a Ramblin' Man* for a gentleman by the name of Waylon Jennings.

Charlie had sent the record off to Mr. Pennington with our contact information, knowing that such packages were sent by the hundreds to major players such as he, but for some reason, Charlie took the chance, never knowing if it would be received by the music giant or not. There were many singers; most, of course, more established, polished, and experienced than me, who were beating down the doors of producers like this, but, when my dad called the number, Ray Pennington answered the phone.

Mom, Sis, Allan, and I sat in astonishment as Dad described his conversation with the Nashville kingpin. To be honest, I really don't recall my initial thought, I'm sure there wasn't one, but many. Excitement, as well as a feeling that it wasn't real, but more than anything, I am sure, there was absolute panic.

Never dithering with his calm and methodical approach, Dad quickly planned the trip with the notorious producer, and the recording session was booked for Wayne Warner, Hilltop Studio's, Nashville Tennessee.

I remember packing the Studebaker but recall little about the twenty-four-hour ride to Music City. I was—surprisingly, given how green I was—focused on the songs that we would be selecting for the session. Even though I was very underdeveloped as a singer, I was conscious about song content, style, and individuality. Of the songs coming out of the radio speakers that appealed to me, it was not so much the "singers" but the "artists" that I was drawn to.

Johnny Cash was my dude. After only one note had danced across his vocal cords, you knew who it was. Many of the "singers" coming out of the dashboard speakers sounded the same to me, making it hard to tell one from the other. I also wanted songs that were age appropriate and that was going to be a challenge. At that time, if you were a sixteen-year-old long-haired boy with tight jeans and you listened to country music, you didn't tell anybody.

We met the renowned producer as well as a song publisher at his office two days before the session. The soft-spoken southern drawler made me feel at ease immediately. Across the walls of his office hung several gold records and photos of the man I now sat across, many of them featuring the great singers we had listened to on our journey from Vermont.

Ray packed tobacco in his pipe as he explained about one particular photo and his long-time friendship with actor John Wayne. I was lost in the wonder of this new world.

There was little time for wonderment. One of Ray Pennington's assistants began the task of playing song after song that they had pre-selected for me from their staff of writers. I liked most, loved none, but I trusted these guys knew what they were doing, and the session was booked. I had four songs that I needed to learn in two days. In the camper, I played those cassettes over and over until the big day.

Dad had the directions and found his way to Hilltop Studios. The massive white structure at the top of the long, paved driveway that had large doors that opened to a universe I had never seen the likes of. The huge band room had vocal booths, large boom mics, headphones galore, and stacked guitar amps. Through soundproof doors the large, dim lit control room had a long couch that lined the entire back wall, and the mixing console was as big as the stage at Buzzy's Barn Dance with what seemed like a thousand knobs. Sitting behind it was Ray Pennington and his recording engineer. I was at a loss for words while at the same time hoping I knew the ones for the songs that we were about to record.

Through the soundproof doors of the studio, the musicians for my session began to file in. They seemed so casual about the event that was about to take place. Didn't they know we were about to make a record? Soon, they were all at their places behind their instruments, and Ray walked me to the vocal booth. He stood me behind the mammoth microphone, handed me my headphones and said, 'You're here because I like how you sing. Now, relax, and sing like you're in your living room.' Nice words, are you F**king kidding me?

Ray Pennington did what he was famous for. While we—with our out-of-state innocence and amateur ignorance—didn't know it, I was blessed by the God my Mama prayed to, with musicians that were session-player royalty. Drummer, Larrie Londin, counted down the first song as pedal steel guitarist phenomenon, Buddy Emmons, played the intro licks to the track. Larrie had pounded the beats on records with everyone from Elvis to Dolly, from the Supremes to Emmylou. Buddy Emmons recorded with legendary artists including Linda Ronstadt, The Everly Brothers, and The Carpenters, to name just a few. Ray would coach me through my monitors and when that band kicked off the song, country gold came through my headphones.

I've been around awhile, and learned a few things. It seems that no matter how hard we try, we can't ever get a "now" back. But that "now" would be one of those that I wish I could.

The music sounded like it had jumped right off the Grand Ole Opry stage and right into my head, and was waiting for my voice to find its mark. When background singer, Janie Fricke, joined me on the chorus, my world as I knew it melted away to the size of a three by three glass vocal booth. My underdeveloped voice located most of the notes and landed somewhere near Larrie's perfect timing. Four songs completed and the session was a wrap. The ride home echoed the Studebaker interior, with excitement about the experience and plans of a new world. I was not elated with the choices of songs and internally committed to two things: I would start to write my own material, and I wanted to know what all those knobs on that mixing board were for. Even though I was only experiencing the early embrace of the industry, I was acutely aware of the fact that I never wanted to turn over control of this part of my life to anyone. Not fully. Not ever.

Chapter 9

Big Machines

In 2005 and getting ready to shoot the video for "Turbo Twang." I had come a long way since that first session in Nashville. I had made a lot of recordings and had learned much about the ways of my new world. One such lesson was media games and how to play 'em. Now, fact is often a myth in show biz. Truth is usually locked up tighter than a set of legs at the monastery. Understand dear friend, It's not lying, its "spin." I have used the spin zone many times. In fact, sadly, in so many cases in entertainment, the truth is not welcomed by the industry nor by the masses. Some of the "spins" are damn cool to read about. Especially, if you were there, and well aware of the story … pre-spun.

The new label venture between Toby Keith and Scott Borchetta didn't last beyond the honeymoon and it …. was a short trip. Scott was signing new artists left and right, but Toby wanted to initially focus on his own new releases. Toby and Show Dog Nashville took all but the furniture and moved out of the office, leaving Scott with a dream and a skeleton crew as well as some of the initial investment money Toby had put down.

Borchetta shifted his focus to putting his side of the merger, Big Machine, on the Music Row map, and it was beginning to work. He built a stellar radio promo team who were plugged in to all regions of the country and began the recording process for his new acts. While a few of the fresh artists on the label struggled, others started to build a name for themselves, and by association, the label.

One young singer who he had signed was creating a buzz that was louder than the others. There are many spins told about how her "discovery" was made. Most are pretty much bullshit. She was a fresh young thing, as cute as she was talented, who came with a lot more than just those amazing qualities. A part of her package was a great new manager—Frank Bell—with inside knowledge of radio, and the connections that came with it. With Frank came the thick wallet of my label partner Ray Pronto. Borchetta needed both the act and the wallet. A star was sure as hell soon to be born. And most of the small crew from the set of the Turbo Twang video shoot were about to make recording history. And that, dear friends, is a story that until now, my immediate family and I, and the ones initially in the room, have celebrated very quietly.

The Big Machine gears kicked in and work began on Taylor Swift's first album on the new label. At the same time and knowing little about Frank and Ray's growing involvement with Big Machine, my bus rolled on. The small team was steadfast as always and did their best to keep our own machine moving forward, but the guy behind the mic was growing weary.

Dad, Unc, Lisa, and Sis were always in and on their game. The other key player on our team, and now Big Machine's new money guy, Ray Pronto, is another true hero of mine, and I am so grateful that I introduced him to the music business. Encased in his name is a rags-to-riches story that deserves a book of its own, and I hope someday he'll write it. He could turn copper to gold, do it with elegance, and help his neighbors along the way—a rarity in any business arena. He was sure about to help make a lot of gold for Big Machine—gold records and their weight in currency—and I celebrate it and him.

I think it was Ray and Sis who began to detect the initial change in me, even before I did. I was turning down shows, telling Juanita not to book that interview. They would press and I would do enough to satisfy, at least for a while, but something was wrong. No matter how good the make-up artist, something in the mirror was starting to fade. The spotlight was waiting, but the flame in my eyes had burned out. There had been too many battles, too many lows. Too many successes, too many highs, miles of highways: ups, downs, and across. The ride was, well, what it was, – was time to roll. Always time to roll.

For me, I had sung, done the act, and performed myself empty, and it seemed like it had been forever. I had lost my vision, even my love for the music. I had been tainted by the business. The pressure of "spin gains per week" at radio; vying for chart position; has the song reached its peak, and is the next single strong enough? Is it ready to go? Is the band happy at all times in their professional and personal lives? Did I get enough miles in on the treadmill this week to be sure my ass was warranted grab-worthy, even if I would never allow security to permit it? This is showbiz, after all. – but oh yeah; then there's music. It was once my only companion in my old bedroom. It was my solace, my sanity back home after those dreadful days of school. I had lost my old friend.

The studio, however, would rejuvenate me. In there, it was about the music and I loved it. The creativity, watching my songs come out of my little cassette recorder and jump to life out of those huge studio monitors, and they came at a volume you could feel. The great studios always had comfy lounges for the artists and the musicians and in those, I spent a lot of downtime with the likes of Bob Seger and George Jones or sharing a pizza with Garth Brooks. It was always great to hang with those guys and learn the secrets of survival of the trade. I did learn a few and being in their presence was always a hoot. Almost all the artists I have worked with were truly inspirational. The camaraderie among them as well as their respect and admiration for each other was something that was such a reward to be a part of, and I was always welcomed by them in whatever venue we shared. For me, that was an especially great and essential gift.

Once in a while, if one of the musicians I knew were playing at the Opry, I would tag along just to be on the sacred turf. Beginning in 1925 as a one-hour "barn dance" radio show on WSM, the broadcast turned a nation on to a new sound. Soon, young dreamers were coming from miles around with hopes of taking a bow from the famous stage. Stars were born and the "Show That Made Country Music Famous" has become the longest running radio show in US history; making Nashville the capital of the genre. For me, just being in the place was always a great opportunity to absorb whatever knowledge I could from the performers. To me, backstage and behind the curtain was where the real show was being played out. The environment held a certified fascination and an undeniable appreciation instilling the knowledge that you were walking hallowed halls.

There's an enchanted feeling behind those curtains. An energy that has a resonance of its own. Perhaps from the distinguished voices of the past as they blend with the vibrations of those who have tuned a multitude of assembled strings. It was a controlled and benevolent kind of chaos, that rendered the atmosphere thick with excitement and energy that seemed to carry a sweet and breezy spirit. Quick last-minute rehearsals would be playing out in the many dressing rooms, and songs fresh off the charts would be bouncing off the walls in live, raw, unplugged form.

On one such night, I happened to find myself standing off to the side of the stage with a man I recognized from my television set. From behind the curtain, we watched the performance playing out in front of the audience and I turned and introduced myself to the *Rhinestone Cowboy* himself, Glen Campbell. I had heard his songs and seen his movies. I had read about his struggles and—more importantly—his victories as they played out in the rag mags at the check-out counters. Living a life of sobriety myself, I felt a connection and a sense of great respect for the man. It's especially sad and unfair when these personal life challenges have to be played out in headlines. My reverence for him, however, went beyond the fact that he had kicked the devil's ass. As a singer I admired him, as I had gained some insight from around the Row that made me understand the extreme intensity of his vocal talent.

While "doing lunch" one day with Harold Shedd to discuss an upcoming meeting, another record producer, a friend of Harold's, dropped by the table to say hello. Harold always seemed to draw a crowd at such venues, and this day was no different. I didn't know who the guy was, but the reminiscing between the two was soon underway. I always appreciated hearing about how the old hits were made, especially from those who were critical factors in creating them. Talk turned to tales about Glen and how he would be delivered to a recording session after a time of over-indulgence. With a couple of musicians under each arm, Glen would be carried into the studio and laid onto a couch with a vocal mic set up next to it, so the story went. They would position headphones on his head, push the red button and Glen would sing songs the likes of *Wichita Lineman* and *Galveston* laying there in a semi-conscious condition. He would hit the notes flawlessly. I fear little contradiction from many of my peers in saying that a lot of us would have a hard time singing like he did on his records; if we had gone to church on Sunday; the day before the session; had hit the sack early; got up and did a 30 minute work-out, and was behind the mic standing in an upright position … just say'n.

I didn't bring that old story up to Glen that night, so I never did confirm it, but if true, then this guy knew how to manipulate vocal chords to the tune of many gold records, even while fighting demons that know how to execute a battle.

Later diagnosed with Alzheimer's, Glen and his family did fantastic things to bring attention to the disease and helped many the world over relate to the common heartbreak that surrounds it. Through Glens' grace, a documentary was chronicled depicting the progression of his illness and the exposure brought understanding to a huge audience.

His family displayed the challenges and the rewards of being caretakers and did so with wit and with love. Glen, like so many, championed us to battle a disease that must be eradicated and having a little hang-time with the man that night at the Grand Ole Opry was a true honor.

Radio touring was extreme, and the station hosts were always an absolute blast for us no matter what state we were in. Sis was immaculate with the scheduling and it was tight and intense. Dad, Unc, Lisa, or sometimes Charlie would call "ETA 15 minutes" from the driver's seat which meant that's all the time Sis and I had to get into "star mode". Juanita would research the area where I would be going on the air, know the names and a little background of the deejays and program directors, and we were "on." Sis would tune the station in about fifty miles before our arrival and you would hear them playing my songs and talking about my upcoming interview. Those always went well, but we would soon be back on the bus and just coming down when we would again hear "ETA 15 minutes" and do it all again. How the team ever put this together and got it down on time, I will never know, but after three to four weeks—from sun up to sun down—it became exhausting, and we truly lost track of where we were and where we had been. This part of the gig, while demanding, was something I was able to appreciate because in this arena, the music was my friend. It had done its job before I even got there. These radio stations were supporters because of my music, and it had already made the introduction. It wasn't the performance, I didn't have to sell, well … me.

Concerts were different, and the ones I couldn't wiggle out of were secretly beginning to take their toll. I don't often read things that were written about me or any of the interviews I had done, but I was starting to see quotes about the "unconventional" or "withdrawn" artist. I asked someone what the words meant. I was beginning to hear voices on stage, mine I'm sure, but they weren't part of the setlist. My band leader, Scott Fowler, who went on to work for Miranda Lambert and Garth, had my band tight and rocking. But Sis, Scott, and Unc could sense that my stage mask was cracking and would carry me through the weak spots when needed. I would do as I often did and stare into the spotlight until I was totally blinded and just find my notes. *Just stare into the light, Wayne, stare into the light.* Unc, especially, who had watched me grow up on stage, was able to make the show appear flawless when in fact, it wasn't. The standing ovations were for me, but to me, it really was for them. At that point, and even at that lower to mid and growing level of success, and with a few "somewhat" hits, I was feeling like a tired and make-believe knick-knack that had been created.

'Sis, when are we going home?'

'Not yet, ETA fifteen minutes.'

Chapter 10

Dadhood

"You're my piece of heaven on Earth
You're my flow'n river, when I'm dying of thirst
The rest of the music to an unfinished verse
You're my piece of heaven on Earth."

– *My Piece of heaven on Earth*, Wayne Warner

I'm a songwriter, I read books, I like language and use it as a living to some degree, but that three-letter word, "dad", that's my favorite. Period. It took becoming one to realize that moms have the most important job in the world—I salute you. I say "dadhood" because I really think that there are WAY too many mothers and fathers on the Earth, not enough, moms and dads, I strive, to be a "dad."

In my early teens, I had seen a documentary about an orphanage overseas. It made a huge impact on me, the kind that leaves a mark on the inside. It paraded the children getting dressed in their very best, as a potential mom and dad were coming to size them up along with all the others, to see if they would be the lucky one to be picked. Maybe, in a very small way, and one much more trivial, I could relate. It showed closeups of tears coming to their young eyes as they were passed by, while still trying to hold a smile. Others, too many of them, were reaching out from a line of cribs, waiting for a pair of arms to bring them close. Wow, I didn't know such places existed, or that the need was so severe, but I did know internally, on that night, that when I was ready to become a dad, it was going to be a set of beautiful eyes from one of those cribs that was going to make me one.

Sandy and I, while never officially married, had been together since she was sixteen and I was twenty. I fell in love with her because she was beautiful, and having moved to Vermont from Connecticut, had never heard of Wayne Warner, at least, not the one on the radio.

As far as Sandy and I knew, we could have "biological" children but we both agreed on adoption and when I was twenty-nine we began the process of becoming a mom and dad. A few months later, and quicker than we could have made one of our own, we got the call we had been waiting for. Our four-month-old bi-racial son was going to be flown by the agency from Miami, Florida to Burlington, Vermont.

We were as nervous, scared, and excited as parents at a hospital delivery room as we waited for the wheels of the plane to hit that tarmac. The second my son, Kyle Jordan Warner, and I locked eyes and I held that boy, my life was changed. It was altered in a way that I could never dream, and words too anemic to define. Songs on the radio, record deals, my photos on bedroom walls, yeah, sure that was neat. But this—this boy's little hand was squeezing my pinky and I never knew such energy could travel through the smallest of fingers, or any finger. That shock wave hit my head and my heart like a thousand volts that welded into my soul. For the first time, I saw and felt what the truest, deepest love was, and for the first time, at that airport, in my son's eyes, I saw the one my mama prayed to.

Five amazing years of dadhood later, Sandy and Sis boarded a plane for Chicago. In the Windy city at two days old, Kyle's brother Keenan was waiting for his new mom and his Auntie Juanita to bring him home. Kyle and I, with my mom's help, waited in Vermont for the big arrival.

We had little background on either of our sons, but Keenan was beautifully black, and the brothers' bond was immediate and forever.

My initial feelings when I first saw Kyle were now, with my two sons, more than doubled. Seeing these brothers together, growing inseparable, one hurting when the other did, wanting always to be side-by-side, and me, vying for the middle, was proof of a plan larger than mine. I know little about fruits and loins, but these boys were and are the trees to my soul. While they didn't grow me taller, they grew me deeper, deeper into what real love, and the meaning of life was all about.

It sounds crazy now, but at that time, ours was the only racially-mixed family known in the area. Our little Vermont town embraced the blend with loving arms. In fact, many of the younger kids in the area had never actually seen a "real black" child before and thought it beyond cool. We were once approached by a little voice who, after seeing Kyle squealed, 'Wow, is he related to Michael Jordan?'

We really developed a sense of humor and have a lot of fun with our blessing of a mixed-race family. Knowing now that some people are sensitive about race, we let them know immediately how proud and at ease we are, and how we are simply the family we were meant to be.

With my sons came a new drive, a new direction, and I tucked my reasons in every night. Something changed. It changed the way I sang, it changed the songs I would sing, and the way I would steer the pen when I wrote them. I was an artist, yes, but now, I was a dad first, and if I couldn't sing songs to my boys that I was proud of, then the lyrics weren't going to cross these vocal cords. Yes, I was country, and still wanted it to be the kickin' ass kind, but the beer slingin', cheatin' songs were being covered. I didn't need to chase that bone. I spent many days ripping pages out of my hook book. Daddy was changing his tune.

With my sons also came the reality that I had a hole I could never fill, and friend, had I tried. But now I knew it was a God-shaped hole, not a religious one. It was a faith-shaped cavity that I knew had to be satisfied, and my boys were helping to pack the void. Okay, God, the one who crafted these masterpieces and let me call them my sons, I don't know you well, haven't read your bible from cover to cover nor has my ass worn the varnish off the church pew, but you're pretty cool and I will, and I do, honor you. Now, can you make it so I can sing better in the mornings?

At some point on one of our many flights back and forth to Nashville, I shared a seat next to a smartly dressed and articulate middle-aged woman. Somewhere in mid-flight, she talked about her grandkids and the pictures started flying. I scanned the photos of her little cuties and reached for my ever-ready pics of my pride and joys. She said they were handsome and that she "didn't see color." I didn't say anything, but I wish I had. I wish I had said, 'What a shame, because the God I pray to makes beautiful colors. He displays them in the rainbows of the skies and in the splendor of his paint, he wraps his souls on the Earth.' How sad it must be, to be that kind of color-blind that just doesn't acknowledge the rainbows on the ground as well as the ones that arch. Or worse yet, when color… blinds the heart. I was soon to learn more about that.

Chapter 11

The Major Leagues, Games and Michael Jackson

"I wouldn't take a million dollars for the honor and the experience of being on a major label, but I wouldn't give a nickel to do it again." Wayne Warner

That was a quote that graced the front page of *Billboard* magazine by none other than yours truly. My dad says sometimes that I don't think before I speak—I sure as hell did before my big lips put those words through 'um.

After making my first few records, it was imperative to me that, right or wrong, an absolute, no discussion reality, was that I had to make the records that I wanted to make. Now, it took many recordings to nail down exactly what that was. To make my sound my own, took years in fact, and am glad to know it's still happening, but after many sessions and continuing to engrave my vocal signature and production style, I began to know what studio guys worked for me and who would break the traditional rules. I was surely the country my daddy raised me on, but I wanted it to be my own and to slop all over the edges. I ended up befriending and utilizing players that graced the hit records of Cougar and Ronstadt, of Elton and Stewart but, mixed in the famous pickers of Emmylou and Haggard. With my music there was no in-between. You loved it or you hated it, but you loved it or hated it—a lot. School days had taught me this: I didn't fit in many places, but these grooves I damn well owned—melody, lyrics, and all.

Borrowing from our family's adventurous business background and successes, a few years earlier, we had formed our own label, appropriately called B-Venturous Records. I know of, and have heard about, the many singers who wait around hoping to be discovered. I guess some have, but that wasn't for me. If I was going to be signed, I wanted the label to know what they were getting so we at B-Venturous, made MY records. Celebrity was not appealing to me, but I, of course, was not wise enough to know that success meant "celebrity." I started to jokingly refer to myself, or at least the "myself" in the press as "WW." He was attaining goals beyond mine, I just wanted to make music that I believed in and knew that through it my persona "WW," would help to give the uncomfortable "Wayne Warner" a voice.

But, the giver of the gift and the one Mama prayed to had other plans. Sis had done her networking and the Row had started to take notice of B-Venturous Records and their flagship artist. First came a few promising meetings with Arista. They were on a roll at the time with Alan Jackson, Brooks and Dunn, Pam Tillis, and a few others. Talks played out for four to six months, but the excitement concluded, mainly due to my desire for creative control. It was made clear to me that a demand such as this from a new artist was practically unheard of. Oh … Okay.

Somewhere in this timeframe, it was suggested by a label that I go into the studio with a well-known producer. I had serious reservations about this, but these people giving the advice knew what they were talking about, right?

The label wanted to hook me up with Nelson Larkin. Nelson had been another one of the Row hit-makers and I liked him within seconds.

I never saw him smoke a cigar, but he sure chewed through a lot of 'em. Meetings were had, songs were picked, and the session booked at the legendary Scruggs Recording Studio. The coveted double-A list musicians that Nelson had slated for the day were also legendary. Stuart Duncan brought his famous violin and had traded licks on records with the likes of Mark Knopfler, Barbra Streisand, George Strait and many more and was laying it down. Reggie Young had played on some of the later Johnny Cash and Merle Records and was guitar royalty. Owen Hale kept the beat and was in town when he wasn't out drumming for the Lynyrd Skynyrd band. Those guys were among the best. That damn record was finished with the perfect Nashville sound and came off as shiny and squeaky clean as everything that was spinnin' on every radio station turntable across the country. Eeee … Yup, and I hated it. They sure as hell knew what they were doing, they just didn't know what to do … with me.

Back to my own sound and with a few more impressive charting positions by B-Venturous and Wayne Warner, we started to gain more attention by the mega players, and Sis began getting more calls from the 615-area code. Renowned music critic Robert K Oermann was practically calling WW a genius with everything I put out, and we could feel the buzz. Additionally, whenever Sis wanted to get in touch with one of the big shakers, well glory be, they would say, 'Why yes, Juanita, they're in today. Hold please.' Funny how things work.

Soon, another major label seemed to be catching the WW groove. I mean REALLY? Dayumn! Trips and talks were plenty. I was uneasy but wasn't sure why. Just like, the big glass buildings, the limos in the yards. Just uneasy. I would ask Juanita many times – many times, 'Sis, do we belong here?' She was something to see in that element. She shined and she loved it. She absolutely belonged there. I should have asked, 'Do I?'

Apparently, talks with the label were going well. Sis had done her thing and my dedication to my sound—whatever that was—was paying off. The label wanted a showcase for all their extended branches. They would fly in their people from New York and California for the show, to hear their potential new Nashville dude. I was used to being watched and stared at, but I was damned sure that I was not going to appreciate being sized-up and studied. But this was the big time—this was a major deal—what everyone was supposed to want. I heard all the singers I had met on the road talk about it: Oh Wow! The Big Time. More radio. All the way, baby!

'Sis, do we belong here?'

The date was set and again, we did it right. We brought in my studio players, the guys who made the hit records, and my records. The sound system was fired up and the light show set up. The place was an intimate setting right down to the ice sculptures carved in the form of my logo. I do know enough about me to say that I'm sure I was nervous, but I really don't remember. Nor do I recall the setlist, what I wore, or who was there.

I do recall a lot of pre-show introductions, freshly lifted smiles and a large crowd. As always, I confirmed that Sis had placed the large 11 x 14 photo of my sons next to my floor monitor and waited for my intro. I hit the stage and the pros behind the strings started playing and the beat was on. Hell, I remember thinking that they were sounding even better than the record. Again, the many Saturday nights that I had stood on the stage my dad built was accompanying me and I once again managed to get the crowd where I wanted them, and I guess in this case, where I needed them, right? The champagne was flowing, whitened teeth were glistening, and the crowd was rocking. It looked like the Vermont boy was about to join the big roster. And then …

It wasn't part of the plan, I hadn't even considered it, although I'm not sure why. It wasn't written on my stage notes or suppressed in my thoughts. I had always tried to use the platform my career would give me to make a difference, to make it matter. And right there before the last song, *I Can Love You from Here*, I bent down and grabbed the photo of my sons. I said, 'These are my adopted boys.' I only mentioned adoption to bring awareness to the great need for the cause—other than that, the word means nothing to me. They are simply, or should I say greatly, my sons. Then I said through the cranked sound system, 'Don't they look just like me?' I expected exuberant laughter from the room but nothing – silence, the kind of stillness you have to paddle through if you want to get to the door.

I know now how clueless I was, but I was stunned and confused. I stood there on the stage with my guitar, in a crowd of people in absolute silence. I really didn't know what was wrong. Still baffled, I stumbled through the last song, got a few tapped claps and was escorted backstage by Sis and whoever our co-manager was at the time. Sis was shaken. I said, 'Juanita. WHAT is wrong? I thought we rocked?' She was upset, she was hesitant, and I, was freaking. *What the hell?* She and co-manager explained that we had an "issue."

The label had asked for and received some background information about me: where I was from; my age (which was always lied about); musical, and family history etc. But, damned if I didn't forget to mention that my amazing sons, the stars of MY life, oh yeah—were black.

Now, the label explained that it wasn't THEM who had a problem with it whatsoever. But, the record-buying demographic could be "funny about these things." 'Perhaps,' they said, 'we could just go with "you don't have any kids"?' I was more than hurt. I was mystified and I was pissed. The words that came out of my mouth have never been typed on the keyboard from which I am tapping, nor will they be now. But the clearest ones I spoke were, 'Sis, please get me on a plane—NOW.' I had NO intentions of ever going back to Nashville, Tennessee.

The next few months were a blur. To go from that high to that low, not only career-wise, but emotionally and spiritually. While I never thought it possible, with this event, I cherished my sons even more, and as always, their young and huge hearts grounded me. In them, I saw, held, and kissed goodnight what I had read about in our history books—the challenges that mankind had overcome. I understood the anger that I had heard about when the color of one's skin can limit the doors that are opened, or closed to you. I perhaps comprehended in a way that only a mixed-raced family could. But, here I was, one of the whitest guys you will ever see, and I was rejected due to skin color. Yeah, damn right. I understood a lot now, for sure. And, I prayed hard, I prayed really hard, for my beautiful sons and everyone like them … or not.

My sons were young then, and we never talked about our experience with the label to them or to anyone else. WW was just "taking a break." At some point later, much of the public laughed when the mass media ran headlines about Michael Jackson calling a division of the label "racist." They snickered, I didn't. I really thought about, and should have gone to his defense. More stories emerged, not only from the recording side of its organization, but from the motion picture arm as well, involving Denzel Washington and others. Later, many firings took place within the company due to racial slurs relative to then President Barack Obama.

Stare into the light, Wayne. Stare into the light. Oh … Okay.

Chapter 12

To Thine Own Self, and Art, Be True

The only lights I was needing at that point said "Good night, Daddy" and "I love you." And wow, as any parent would know, they lit my world and still do. But, I confess that the home front, as much as I loved and needed it, was foreign to me after a while. I needed to sleep with a window fan because I was used to the hum of the road, as the bus would rock us to sleep at night. Also, whenever we would cross the immediate town line and out of what really became the shelter of my amazing neighbors, people would begin to recognize me; the whispers, the pointing, the, "Can I have a picture?" The boys became very accustomed to this, but for me, I was supposed to be home. I didn't want to be "on." I wanted to be Dad.

A neighboring town was hosting their annual Field Day. This was a great community event focused on local kinship, family rides, and candy. It was a big deal in the very rural Vermont woods. The boys were excited; their dad was home, and we were all going to go. We got as far as out of the car. The boys were so kind and patient and lightly tugged at my hands to head for the rides as I posed for pictures with this one, that one, and then, another. Finally, I told the family I would be back to pick them up later. My heart was breaking as I watched them. They were so excited for the rides, couldn't wait to see the animals, and get some fried dough. I was smiling, but the rear view mirror got blurry as I watched them go through the gate. My sons were—they are—my world. *Where do we go now?*

Sis, do I belong here?

Sis was as lost as I was. In fact, I think Juanita missed the road and the showbiz scene more than I did. She needed to be back on 16th Avenue, Nashville, Tennessee. She wasn't herself here at home, and to be honest, except for our amazing town friends and neighbors, nobody really knew how to relate to us anymore, and on some level, neither did we. But, at least when we were in the chaos, and we got the standing ovations, it really didn't matter. We needed to hear, she needed to hear: ETA to somewhere, anywhere, 15 minutes.

I was angry. I had been disillusioned by the industry; the highs and the lows, by the games that were played with the lives of people and all with impunity. I had been bullied so much. Too much. Enough! I'm stronger now … right?

I don't know who suggested it – or, if I pursued it on my own, but I knew that if I was going to go back to Nashville, there was only one person I had to have a conversation with first.

Due to topic sensitivity and respect, I will not mention his name, but many will know. Back at Buzzy's barn dance, my dad sang those old hit songs. Some of my favorites were made hits by a man who, when his first album was released, was done so without his picture on the cover. He scored hit after country hit before anyone ever discovered that he was black. He was also one of the first black musicians to ever grace the Grand Ole Opry stage and I needed to talk to him. I needed some understanding, or to talk to someone who understood.

Bob Heatherly, a longtime Nashville label player and mutual friend, made the call possible. The talk was short, and he was incredibly gracious. As incredible and gracious as he could be while at the same time asking me, "where ta Hell ya been all your life that you would be ignorant to such issues on this scale?" A man of faith and love, he said something simple, a long-distance call, short and powerful, from a man who had fought the fight, or didn't – and won anyway. My dad had sung his words so many times and now the man himself spoke directly to me and said, 'Sing, Mr. Warner. Just sing. The rest will fall into place.' Wow! I was amazed and will forever be grateful to this soul, for giving mine the music back. I never spoke to him again.

Sis was on the phone booking our flights to the Nashville airport. The studio and the musicians were scheduled for a new recording session. I had been writing. Hank Williams Sr. had often been quoted for saying "God writes the songs, I just hold the pen". I had been holding the pen a lot. I'm not sure whether God would want the co-write credits for all of them or not, but I always did my best. I think I am remembering correctly when I say that it was a day before the recording when famed bassist and my session leader Dave Pomeroy called to inform me that my usual lead guitarist could not make the session, but not to worry. He had booked a guy that would be fantastic.

I worried anyway. I had faith in Dave, and anyone who listens to country or mainstream radio has felt his low-end grooves many times, but I was concerned. I had chemistry and a long-time rapport with my usual cast of pickers. I knew that I was vulnerable if I strayed or was pulled too far out of my element in any forum.

My concerns lasted no longer than it took for Troy Lancaster to hit the first set of licks on track one. This guy got me and my sound immediately and took it to a whole new level. We became fast and close friends, something I would seldom allow. That session, and the ones to follow with Troy's co-production, another thing I had never endorsed, got attention and got it fast—this time, from the guy that everyone in the business knew well, Harold Shedd. He had been deputized as a musical genius by his own successes and there were many. He was Nashville's answer to pop's Clive Davis. Clive had produced or discovered pop and rock superstars that ranged from Joplin to Springsteen, from Aretha to Whitney, Billy Joel and many, many more.

Shedd brought to audiences what was called "The Artists of The Decade." He discovered, signed, and produced a little unknown band when all the people that "knew better" told him what a mistake it would be, that it would never work, that "the band didn't have what it took." Harold produced, financed and released the project himself. The band, Alabama, who "didn't have what it took" took thirty-three records to number one and sold seventy-five million albums.

The trend was set for Harold, who signed and/or produced Toby Keith, Billy Ray Cyrus, Shania Twain, KT Oslin, and many more that you could sing along to. At this point, you don't call Harold Shedd, Harold calls you, and that's if he wants to. Sis answered the phone.

Gold records filled the walls and a huge portrait of the iconic producer hung over a massive stone fireplace in the secured lobby. More gold wallpapered the staircase that led to his second-floor office. Framed posters were autographed by Sonny and Cher, Alabama—of course—and many mainstream artists of yesterday and today. All signed with thanks to the man.

Sitting there waiting to be called up the multitude of steps, I, for the first time ever, had a moment of satisfaction, of quiet from all the negative tones of the past. Being invited here temporarily put them on pause. I had asked Garth once what it had felt like to "make it." He replied, 'I'll let you know when I get there.' I know now what he meant, and I don't know the answer either, but sitting there on that stuffed couch sure felt close to wherever "there" is.

I had done my research, and the more I learned, the more I dug this guy Harold. He had done it his way. He had been laughed at too, and he was a victor. He let them chuckle and then he kicked ass—hard. With him, I already knew I would feel a sense of comfort and a connection, and I did. This giant was digging me and my music. Over and above all previous meetings, all other stages, this was surreal.

Sis and I were finally beckoned to ascend the stairs inside the celebrated Music Mill. Harold's loft office was twice the size of my living room and even more gold reflections and signed posters adorned the walls. Harold, well-dressed in casual attire, spoke in a soft and easy drawl. He was sizing me up for sure, but a comfort zone owned the room. He, of course, was a pro with putting people at ease.

Small talk preceded the real reason we were there, and as yet, I wasn't sure what that was. We talked about common friends in the biz and I marveled about the hit records he had made. I noticed immediately that he wasn't one to boast or hang on the topic of his works for too long. I really wanted to hear some of the back-stories behind the mega successes and learn all I could from the master for however many minutes I would be allowed in his presence.

I glanced at the gold plaque of Billy Ray Cyrus's song *Achy Breaky Heart* and shared how many times I had sung it on our home stage. He then explained how the song had almost never happened. He said Billy, from Kentucky, would come into town once a year and for many of those trips, Harold would grant the "overnight success" a meeting, ending with a, 'See ya next year,' send-off. These were the times when the flavors of the day were cowboy hats, creased jeans, and belt buckles you could land a plane on. Randy Travis, George Strait, Garth, and Alan owned the airwaves.

Billy strolled into town with a cut-off T-shirt, faded jeans tucked into high tops and hair mid-way down his back. But Harold, ever the rebel that I loved, saw something in the guy that only Harold could see. Such was the origin of all those granted once-a-year meetings. At some point, a song on a cassette perked ole Harold's golden ears and he linked it to that boy from the Blue Grass State. He set it on his desk to await the Kentuckians' yearly visit. Billy was ecstatic when the producer told him that he found a song he thought might be a fit and told the wannabe star that at some point he would just like to take him into the studio to "see how it goes."

I never knew what the name of that song was, not many do. Billy, his heart pounding with excitement at finally having a chance at achieving his dreams at the bigtime, was listening to the tape over and over on the road home. After listening to the song for many miles, at some point, the tape clicked to the B-side and Billy heard a different song. A guitar riff caught his ear immediately, a song titled *Don't Tell My Heart*.

Once again, Harold was laughed at and at high decibels. This long-haired, no hat, tight jean wearin' guy sure as hell wasn't ever going to be played on radio. 'Especially,' they said 'with a two-chord song from hell.' Really? 'Okay,' said ole Harold.

Don't Tell My Heart, now changed to *Achy Breaky Heart*, sure as hell was played. It was played night and day and was run up the charts like a blur, making Billy Ray Cyrus a megastar that brought the format a whole new generation of ears. *That* was Harold Shedd, and he was talking to me.

Turns out old Harold was tired of dickering with the majors as well. By this time he had been president of a few. Now, Harold was quietly building his own Independent label, Tyneville Records. Well that's cool as hell. With Harold behind it – this will be a site to see. I'm thinking, *Fantastic, cool, awesome,* and I hear my voice saying *inside – to me – so what's that got to do with WW?* But, the voice in my head should have shut up and listened further, and it did.

'I've heard your latest record,' Harold said. 'I would like to talk to you about being Tyneville's first artist. With the exception of one mix change on one song, we would buy the master as-is.' He stated that I was unique and artistically ahead of the curve – where music was headed. I was floored!

This was one of those moments, and you have had them, when all the plans; the ones that you had made and wondered if you were doing right; the ones that kept you up all night and sweating all day; the ones that often implored the question; "Was it worth it?" This is one of the times when all of those "ones" were answered, all in one choir and time with an amplified, "YES!"

Sis was a pro and handled it as such. But the inside of my head felt like twenty major cities had combined their allotted treasures for their annual 4th of July celebration, and the whole damned colossal display was going off in the high school dropout, grey matter of my brain.

But, I was a performer, I learned that, and damn well on my daddy's stage. Fireworks display and all, it was at this very moment, this little Vermont singer's job to sit back and paint the face of nothing more than a BiC lighter that won't catch a spark. "Oh, well Harold, that's cool. So um, yeah, sure Bud, sounds great."

Harold Shedd changed my musical life in such a positive and dramatic way. Positive because when Harold Shedd is a fan of what you do, now THAT is validation, and the "last boy not to be picked" desperately needed it. This legitimacy was coming from Nashville's version of "on high." The "last one not to be picked" had hit one out of the frigg'n music city park. Harold's endorsement would put a rag in the mouths of the negative voices in my head, that along with all the others, who would also question my artistic abilities. Those inquiring little vermin had had their way with me all they were going to. Or, so I thought.

As Juanita drove back to the condo, our minds were racing. I was filled with pride for her, for the family, for Troy, for all the musicians, the engineers and all those at the radio stations. All the collective hearts and souls who had brought me here. I was so grateful for my sons who had said, "Good night, I love you, Dad," and said it way too many times, over the phone. It had always been my name on the album covers, but I was by no means a solo act, and at that moment, the team spirit of unity was overflowing. I was flying home to them now while the lawyers got down to the process of putting together a contract between WW and Tyneville Records.

Sis and I were both proud of Vermont, our home state. The people there, true to their roots, their values, and their dedication to work. Yes, we were grateful to our home and we had brought it here with us. Few from there had taken it here, not to this place, and for now, we were taking our gratitude and boarding a plane once again back to the Green Mountains to wait for our call.

Back on the Warner's Saturday night stage, I again sang *Achy Breaky Heart* and Juanita cranked out Shania Twain, Patty Loveless, and Faith Hill. Weekdays were filled with me and my boys a mile up the hill at the elementary school's basketball court. I would watch them for hours, just the three of us. I had a record deal and my sons by my side, and with them, the picture was complete, and the colors were perfect. Of Course, Music City had more surprises to come.

Chapter 13

Atlantic Waves

We didn't have to wait long for the 615-area code to hit Juanita's cell phone. A call from Joyce at Harold's office informed us that the contracts were ready, and the room was booked in one of the Music Mills studios for a quick fix and remix on one of the songs that the mega-producer wanted to address. On every album I recorded, I was committed to writing and adding a track that paid tribute to the very traditional style of country that I grew up on. It was that one song *Where Forever Ends* that Harold wanted to bring the vocal up in the mix and fix a "pocket" or "timing" issue with the drum track. During the process, I overheard Harold saying to the engineer and above the sound of the speakers, "Wow, that's how you write a song." Coming from this man—the man behind the hits— as a writer, I was elated.

He liked my unique writing style and discouraged me from co-writing, stating that whatever I was doing had an approach that was fresh and unique. I knew that I chased that with production but was surprised that he found that in my crafting of songs. It really was nothing other than trying to write as the pros did and failing miserably. Co-writing was something that I never did pursue. I had a few good writing sessions with someone I first met while we were doing interviews together at the CMA Fest. It took place on Loretta Lynn's tour bus hosted by XM Satellite's Shannon McCombs. With me on that interview was an artist that I was glad to meet. He had scored many great songs and on many labels.

As a songwriter, he was admired by everyone who ever thought about scratching down a lyric and gave George Jones a few more hits with *Choices* and *I Don't Need That Rocking Chair*. Billy Yates kinda took this new kid under his wing that week at my first CMA Fest and I will always be grateful. Any time I get to share a notepad with a master like that, yeah, I'll take it.

As any writer knows, songs are in some ways a 'baby' to us. They come from a deep place within, or in my opinion, they should. Only in this way is it true enough to connect in a deep way with others. I always felt that If I'm gonna make a 'baby' with someone, we need to date for a while first, and I am not much for dating. Nor have I ever been one of those 'briefcase' writers that walk from appointment to appointment for co-writes on a schedule. I have been in the rooms when these happen and when the chemistry is there, it's damn cool. While an approach I rarely engage in, many hits have been born of this method. But, if ole Harold liked what I was doing and the way I was doing it, well, I was just fine with that.

The contracts with Tyneville were signed and the album fixes complete. I was ready to return home to my sons for a few days, as I knew my world was about to get crazy and my time away from them even more frequent.

Sis and I were barely unpacked when the now familiar and friendly Joyce once more called from Harold's office asking us to return to the Music Mill. There had been a change that they wanted to discuss with me. Sis booked a flight.

While I was now smoking nothing more than my cigarettes, I ain't saying nothing new by sharing that ole Harold liked to pack them pipes with something that had a little more kick. The story as I heard it was that he had already packed a few one Nashville night when he invited his pal and Atlantic Records Nashville's head of A&R's Al Cooley over to hear his new 'boy.' Maybe Al took a toke or two himself, but he went nuts over the fresh and unique sound that Harold was cranking. Al begged him to let him bring it to Atlantic's new label head.

Like Harold, Barry Coburn was becoming rare in the music capital in that he was all about the music. Imagine that! And, like me, Barry was a bit of an outsider, but he had done well and had earned a lot of 'creds' in the city. Originally from Australia, he and his wife Jewel had established the very successful publishing company Ten Ten Music. Jewel had grown up in the entertainment field as a child actress appearing in roles on classics like Bonanza, Lassie, and Mod Squad as well as getting major roles in several movies. She also knew her way around a song having been a recording artist for RCA and Capital.

One day in his office, Barry Coburn met a tall fella from Georgia who had come to Nashville like so many with dreams to sing in that famous circle on the Opry stage. Barry heard something he liked and drove him around to be rejected from every 'know-it-all' in town. They finally got to Arista's Tim Dubois. You know, you really have to wonder don't ya? What do all those idiots behind their desks say to themselves when they utter "Nah, the guy just don't have it," and then this happens? Tim Dubois thought the guy had 'it' and immediately got him into the studio to record the song that Barry had him sing in his office. *Here in The Real World* shot to number three on the national charts and Alan Jackson sure as hell sang in the circle.

Barry and Jewel helped to shape our radio waves by nurturing fellow Aussie, Keith Urban, into fame, securing many more radio hits, as well as stretching beyond the banjos to license music for the *Hannah Montana* movie and Selena Gomez's track for the movie *Ramona and Beezus*.

It was no surprise to 16th Avenue when Barry was chosen to fill the void as Atlantic Nashville's new label head, upon the exit of Rick Blackburn. He hadn't even watered his plants in his new office for the first time when good ole Al Cooley buzzed him and said he had a CD he had to hear. It was later at the home of Barry's and Jewel's when the first song off my CD *Love Thing* cranked out of the Coburn sound system, and WW was the initial act the new president of the label wanted to sign. I, of course, didn't know s**t about any of it.

Such was the reason behind sweet Joyce's call from Harold's office asking us to return to the big city. In Harold's office, there were lawyers dancing around like they were trying to put out a leaf fire and papers flying like a Vermont blizzard. To this day, I don't know why all the spaces next to where I was to sign were pre-dated, I guess it doesn't really matter, but before it was over, me and my album had been sold from Harold's Tyneville Records to Atlantic Nashville. I don't know the amount that was written on the check to ole Harold for the sale of my ass, but I was damn happy with the numbers on mine. WELL … the last boy 'not to be picked' was on a roll on this Frigg'n day.

Sis and I had passed the large and gated half-circle driveway at 20 Music Square, East Nashville, many times and we had never even attempted access. But now, I was the new artist that belonged to the building. A division of Time/Warner, Atlantic Records shared record distribution and the second floor of the huge stone and glassed-faced building at Warner Bros. Several meetings were going to take place and I was about to get an inside major view of how the big boys set about the plan for dropping a record on the masses.

Especially rewarding to me was that the mega-label was keeping the record as it was, other than a few more mixing edits by one of Nashville's finest, Kyle Lehning. Kyle had produced almost all of Randy Travis' hit records as well as many others.

I was escorted from office to office, couch to couch. There were meetings with many astonishing people who knew how to go about the business of making songs and singers famous. I met the publicity department, the promotional departments, and Al Cooley's artists and repertoire department. If they were in town, I was introduced to my new label mates, all of whom I sure as hell recognized at first sight by the magazine covers they had graced and the chart action they had scored. Sis and I would often share the lobby space with then Warner Bros artists Dwight Yoakam and Faith Hill as we all waited for our meeting call. I had always found Dwight's personality as one of an artist to the core. Under a baseball cap and behind the scenes, even his language in conversation was lyrical with an in-depth knowledge of music history and with strong opinions on its present-day direction. Time would pass quickly in those comfy couches in the lobby at 20 Music Square.

When it was time to get down to business, plans were made for drop dates for radio ads; album set up; press releases; photo shoots; graphics; and branding. As such, the meeting turned towards image: That is to say – mine. Now see, enter here the part that puts me on edge and in internal conflict. The voice in my head replayed those old school tapes of the discomfited, skinny kid and the taunting I endured. Image was not my friend and any discussion of it brought on a heavy dose of self-consciousness, especially in this new doll-like world my ass was now sitting in. How I had pulled it off to get so far was something I never did understand, and I kept waiting for the secret, whatever that was to give me away. I had been taught by the trade to know how to use a look to stand out and used it when I needed to. Such would give fodder to much conversation and a few double-takes back in the woods of Vermont, that's for damn sure. This confirmed I was doing it right. My home neighbors were astounding with their encouragement and their understanding as I went through the transition from hometown boy to charting artist and always embraced me even if neither they nor I could fully grasp the scale or the dynamics of the complete change of lifestyle.

However, radio wasn't the only pipeline to the record-buying masses that the labels were targeting these days. Videos carried much of the load now as well as the internet employing graphics galore. So it was that Barry sat across the desk to discuss the damn topic of my image.

Now, here also, I have to address the genius of Barry Coburn. Unlike what every other label in town was doing to their new male acts, which was to send them off to the local Hee Haw shop to get a cowboy hat that fits, a pair of pointed boots, and an overly embroidered shirt, he let my music and what he had gathered of my personality direct the plan of attack. He said he wanted to structure me as the label's male version of Shania and added, "We need you to be comfortable, Wayne." Well, that would be a first. If you can pull that sh*t off, I'll buy you another plant for your office! He further explained that I was more cosmopolitan, with regard to image, and that he and the label felt that such a look would fit my brand. As he talked on, I scribbled a note to Sis and slipped it to her. It said this, *Look up the f**king word 'cosmopolitan.'*

Then he said something that scared the hell out of me. He stated that they had me booked on a flight to New York City for a few days to work with an image consultant. Are you kidding me?

The label heads face contorted in a way that its muscles had never been flexed when I said truly, and with the utmost of Vermont charm, "What ta'f**k you talking 'bout? The record's done, take a damn polaroid, slap it in a case, and ship the sum'bitch before rigor mortis sets in for the love of God, lets roll."

The flight to New York was agony made worse by the reality that it was only the second time after hundreds of flights that I was on without Sis. I felt totally lost. I should have been thanking the God my mama prayed to for all that had gotten me here and the unbelievable place my career had taken me. Instead, I was feeling guilty about the fate of the other passengers as I hoped for a drunken flock of geese to soar through our engines before I had to sit with a stylist in the Big Apple.

Image dude, Pieter, was to meet me at LaGuardia for the three-day turnaround of transforming this guy into a magazine cover. THREE DAYS? To do all THAT? Well, maybe the blend of my mama's and daddy's chromosomes didn't do so bad after all, or maybe this guy had a wand. Pieter had groomed and pruned many of the gents that have pranced across our televisions, and now the guy who had helped to dress the likes of Leonardo DiCaprio was going to put my ass in just the right pair of jeans that was supposed to help sell albums. It turns out, the discount shelf at the local Walmart just wasn't going to do. Friend, all this time I had been doing it wrong, I was just trying to write good songs

I've always hated shopping, but Pieter was a pro to the soul at making me feel as comfortable as possible. I still didn't love it, but this guy knew what he was doing and read me like a book. Knowing my level of discomfort, we didn't waste time and he had already done a lot of his homework on me before my plane ticket was even booked. We settled on two shirts and a pair of jeans. When Pieter paid $12,000 for the three items off Atlantic's credit card, I tried to look unimpressed. My heart, however, was in need of the paramedics.

Next, dear image consultant Pieter sized me up a bit more and decided that the next day we would meet with a personal physical trainer. It seemed that my shoulders were a bit too scrawny and I needed a little buffin'. What? Just hand me the mic and kick off the damn song!

The fancy-schmancy gym was locked up tight to those who weren't granted special access and, oh yay, Pieter had it. It was early morning, I hadn't had enough coffee and what's more, the gym didn't have any ashtrays. Apparently, they didn't know how to treat musicians with a damn record deal. I recognized Regis Philbin, the good time morning talk show host, right along with many other 'buffed' bodies I had seen on movie posters. They were pushing and pulling, jumping and squatin', runnin' and rowin'. But hay – that's right, hay. I had thrown a bale or two on a few Vermont farms. Yes, that was years ago, but I hit the damn treadmill every day. Bring it.

The personal trainer looked like the results of a Rambo and Schwarzenegger date that had gone really well. He was as polite as could be and somehow didn't laugh at me as he had me lay down on some contraption to do some 'reps.' Okay, I mean, all of this for the Opry?

By the time I got to the fourth rep, I knew I was in trouble. Where ta' hell was Sis now? There was Regis with his thousand-dollar leotards pressing away and not even breaking a sweat. I was dying, pressing nothing but the bar in those favorite sweats with the holes in them, praying for God to take me. "Three more," said trainer. No way. "C'mon, you can do it." Regis is slamming away. Right then and there, I knew I hated him.

The personal trainer took it easy on me and ran me through a bunch more programs using biceps, triceps, and every other damn muscle under human skin. Finally, he gave me a chart and had Pieter make me promise I would stick to the regimen. Oh yeah, "You got it, Bud." I walked out of there, lit a cigarette and made two promises to myself. I would never lift another barbell or watch f**king Regis and Kathie Lee ever again.

The next morning, I was hurting in places I didn't know I had places. I crawled, I mean, I literally crawled to the sink and while on my knees I put some toothpaste on the brush, held it in place on the counter, and rubbed my teeth back and forth across the sum' bitch.

Luckily, Pieter was wrapping things up today. It was going to be spent in a chair. Thank you, God. Dyed eyelashes, eyebrows, and an eight-hundred-dollar haircut later, I was ready to slap on my Versace shirt, pull my new jeans up on my buffed ass and bring it all back on a plane to Nashville. Okay Atlantic, I'm ready for my close-up. But, there was a glitch, of course. And again, it was not about the music, but the business of it. This sh*t was getting old, but on the plus side, I looked good.

Atlantic's marketing agent had a meeting with Sis and me to discuss the building of the website and whatever arms of social media there were at the time. But, it turns out there are people who make their living by sniffing the air in the 'Ville' to find out what artist is coming down the pike with talks of a label deal. And then, these kind folks buy every .com and .net and register every domain that could be associated with that artist. Sure enough, I no longer owned the name my mom and daddy put on my birth certificate. The guy who did possess my name didn't look or sound anything like me and wasn't surprised to hear from our camp.

Now, anyone who's old enough to read these lines is well aware that in a fast and loud world, there are many difficult situations in life. Some of them grant just cause for an asshole attitude to crawl right up into your soul and visit for a minute, maybe two. But, why anyone would want to give it a lifetime home has always been a mystery to me. However, the guy who owned my name was sure enough in on the damn secret. A few family meetings and $10,000 later, I could once again respond when someone addressed me as Wayne.

Sis had always been my stand-in at social events and everyone became cool with the fact that WW liked to lay low. If anyone wanted anything from me, they knew she was the go-to and she, knowing what was out of bounds with my comfort level, would agree to or not. They loved her and she could schmooze with the best as well as have a social drink or two. A form of socializing for which I could no longer indulge. Like many top positions in most major forums at the time, it was predominantly male-dominated and once, when I was asked by some of the main pen-pushers where she fit in the picture, I said, "You won't find her in the picture, she's the canvas it's painted on." That was the end of that, and she was a part of the team.

Atlantic however, wanted their acts to show up at the Warner Brothers/Atlantic Plaza for the Country Music Awards (CMA) after-party, which meant I was expected. Sis couldn't wait and I confess it was exciting to be summoned to this illustrious event. My name on the invite served as further proof that I had done something right. Holding firm to my beliefs in taking the long way and staying true to the gift as I unwrapped it, had paid off.

The CMA after-party took over the whole of the huge Warner Bros/Atlantic complex including the roof patio. The night was made for it with the stars in the warm night sky shining as brightly as the earthly ones that I was now in the middle of. Limo after limo entered the half-circle drive to deliver the performers and the winners of the night. As much as Barry was in demand, he was sure that I was introduced to all when we were together in proximity, and he was dressed to the max. I felt as out of place as I would have on an NBA line-up, but I had my performance mode running on all it had. Actually, that's about the only part of me in attendance that night that didn't come from New York City. Al Cooley was my biggest fan at the label and thought I could do no wrong. While everyone loved the music man, he didn't seem to like the big hoopla's any more than I did, and quite often he and I were retrieved from hiding in one of the many corners.

I liked label-mate Craig Morgan right away. He had already notched up a few hits and was a country boy to the core. I had met Craig before at one of Nashville's many music clubs. They were hosting a writer's night 'in the round' type performance and Craig was behind the mic. The minute I heard him singing live with nothing but a flat-top guitar and a less than perfect sound system, I was a fan of his talent. The second I met him, I was a fan of the man. His down-home approach to life really helped this far-away-from-home boy that night. Sis was having a ball; this is where she shined. One minute, she was comforting Lee Ann Rimes, who had struggled with her live performance due to vocal strain, and the next, laughing it up with Warner Bros Vice-President and friend, Bob Saporiti. Dwight was there, as were many Warner Bros artists, but there were a few pissed off execs because Faith Hill and Tim McGraw decided to ditch the bash to get burgers at White Castle. Good for them I say.

Finally, after a lot of hours and many drinks of Champagne, we could make our way out to the parking lot. Sis and I had made it. We played the role and pulled it off. They did know how to throw a party, and it was done to the max. We did mention on the ride back to the condo, that the only ones in attendance who weren't white, were wearing white gloves and serving drinks and hors d'oeuvres.

I will say though, to my amazement and to the credit of the label, Atlantic was not only fine with my sons, they agreed to allow me to post a photo of them in the credits of my CD. I had some changes I wanted to make in town, and these astounding people were letting me take the first steps. But, the first steps never scuffed the heels of my boots or moved an inch, at least not for me, not yet, and not on Atlantic Records Nashville.

While Sis and I returned home for family time, the label was beginning its work for setting up the release of my first major label album and the selection of the first single for radio promotion. I was really at ease on that escape back to my sons. I felt what I thought was a sense of exhilaration. Not only the kind always offered from my boys but from a battle won, and a damn long struggle it had been. Odds had always been against us, for sure. Demographics as well as the unheard-of approach that I had taken would often seem a herculean goal. I had spent years in studios writing, and on stages developing my sound, trying to keep my self-assurance and my convictions in balance while keeping up the fight. My family's endurance and my exhaustive will to combat the old voices of negativity in my head had accomplished the impossible. The record was ready, release dates were planned, and I had a label head that was enthusiastic and behind this artist.

But in advance, the record was sent out to those who 'know-it-all.' Their actual titles are more distinguised of course and on their business cards it reads 'radio consultant.' These people didn't know what to make of this 'new and unique' sound that had so captured Harold Shedd and Barry Coburn and felt that it wasn't 'safe' for mainstream radio. By 'safe,' they explained, it just didn't sound the same as 'everyone else.' No f**ing kidding.

When heavy-hearted Barry called me at my Vermont home to tell me the record wasn't going to ship, I was initially shocked and confused. It was only after a few weeks that I had discovered my feelings of absolute relief. Somewhere deep inside, I was still veiling a little boy with messy hair and freckles around his nose. He was hiding behind his guitar in his dad's shadow at Buzzy's Barn Dance. The boy had been through a tough week at school, but he was already a performer and he was smiling. But then of course, smiling as you may know or have experienced yourself, is just how a performer cries, isn't it?

That young boy had also made a promise to himself when he was sixteen on his first return trip home from a Nashville recording session. He committed that he would never turn his career over to the hands of someone else. Not entirely. Such was the cause for the relief of my freedom from Atlantic Records. Proof of good reasoning for such an internal promise was to come in just a few weeks.

The headlines read, "Atlantic Nashville To Close Its Doors." Thirteen employees including Barry Coburn were locked out of the building without warning, and my former label-mates and some new friends including Tracy Lawrence, John Michael Montgomery, Craig Morgan, and others were now musically on the streets.

Aside from myself, Atlantic Nashville had signed one other new solo act. She had paid her dues, served her time, groomed her chops, and had finally made it; her time was here. Atlantic, along with her producer, had finally found the songs, recorded, mixed, and mastered the album. Also, for her, the image work had been done, the photo shoots completed, and albums pressed. Finally, after her lifetime of effort, her moment had arrived and Atlantic Records Nashville shipped her first single to radio, with her right behind it on an extensive and exhaustive radio tour to promote the song. Overjoyed that her moment had finally arrived and while at a radio station and ON THE AIR, a friend called her to tell her that not only had her label closed, but that the Atlantic expense account allotted for her trip had been discontinued. Her family was sending her funds to get home.

I really believe that had Barry Coburn remained at Atlantic's helm with Al Cooley as his wingman and allowed to run it in the direction he was attempting to, he would have been behind some music discoveries we would still be talking about today. But, he was doing it wrong; he was about the music. Go figure.

Chapter 14

Earlier "Sound" Development

"Bring on the beat boys renew my soul
Bring back what time erases
The highs and low notes as we grow
Co-write our stories pages
Rewind the time bring back my glory days
With the songs of my ages."

— *Song of My Ages*, WAYNE WARNER

I'm not sure this chapter belongs in here, but it's a huge chapter of my life as well as the lives of too many musicians we don't know. And, a part of life regarding too many people you do know. I am in hopes that perhaps by sharing my story, it may serve in some small way to change a page or two of yours.

Not long after hearing my record on the radio for the first time ever, my life took a detour into a dark abyss. I've heard that many artists go there; too many have died in the place. I think there's still a little bit in all of us who would still like to hold a crayon occasionally if no one was looking, and that there's a trace of an artist in everyone. But, in working with so many, and perhaps by being one, I have sensed that the bigger the gift, the greater the curse, or at least the perception of such an affliction. Like all, the true and deep artist grows up wanting to fit in and feel 'normal.' But to me, there is nothing 'normal'—whatever the hell that is—about the artist 'type.' Emotionally, they venture to places through their art that most don't. As such, many people love to visit a song, a photo, poem, or painting to see, hear, or feel another dimension for a while. But artists live in these outer worlds, and these places can feel very lonely even when they are in a crowd. Such is the 'curse' part of the gift, or at least, in the view of this humble scribe. It is my opinion that artists dream bigger, love deeper, hurt harder, and cry wetter. Until we learn to accept this as an extension of the gift, many do as I did, or tried to: escape.

Booze, it was never allowed on my dad's stage. It had never had a place in my life except for what I saw of it, and the effects that I had witnessed from behind the mic. Tucked under the arms and in the coolers of all those who crossed the ticket booth at Warner's was every make and kind, and of all sizes. It never appealed to me. I had seen people come in as a family and after sucking down the multitude of personalities encased in those bottles, leave a family destroyed. At the age of seventeen, I guess I would have been considered a late bloomer, and I remember my first taste well. It wouldn't be my last.

We had a new drummer, and for the first time, my dad had to reach beyond the branches of the family tree to fill the beat. I liked the guy. Jim was older than me, but closer to my age. A little more radical with the drum rolls and more might behind the kick drum. I knew we were going to get along just fine.

One very hot summer night, made even steamier on the blistering stage by the large crowd and the pole lighting, I noticed Jim was sipping from his usual red solo cup.

Hidden by his kick drum, I had noticed it often. After singing one of the usual covers and pouring in sweat, the icy beverage was calling. I leaned and said, "Hey, give me a swallow of that would ya?"

He laughed and said, "You really don't want this." I was hot, it was cold, I smiled and said, "Hand it over and count down the next song."

I took a large gulp of whatever it was, but sure as hell knew it carried a punch the second it hit the back of my throat. My eyes burning, I hit the mic and launched into the next melody. By the next set, even though not one more soul had slid another dollar across the ticket booth, the crowd had grown twice in size, and I was sounding twice as good. At least, I was to me.

With one drink, all inhibitions were swallowed with the booze. Not a single insecurity whispered in my ear. I was in the here and now and listening to nothing but my voice singing *My Maria* and I was 'on.' Before I knew it, the last song was played, and I was walking across the parking lot to our house next door. I couldn't wait for next Saturday night and Jim's red solo cup.

At that time, I did manage to finally have a few weekday buddies. In my small town, there were three other high-school drop-outs. The title granted me membership into the club and they did welcome me out of boredom and needing to up their numbers if nothing else. The association brought me into a world I had never witnessed. The bond these three had formed as they had grown up together, all around the corner from me but a world away, was something I was immediately envious of. Together, they had shared winning scores, the loss of loved ones, teenage romance, and virgin heartbreaks. I know now the depth of their innocence, but then, and in woodsy rural Vermont, they were rebels. They smoked, they drank, swore, and scored with the girls whenever they could.

Scott, Patrick, and Brad had awakened me to a planet that was spinning on a different axle than mine, and theirs was surely a lot dizzier. I laugh about it now, but the first time I saw them roll a joint and smoke it in front of me; I was speechless. This was something I had heard about, but it sure as hell wasn't in my peripheral. I felt like I was watching a movie and I'd somehow been sucked into the screen. They smoked the skunk weed stolen from the local hippy's shack on the hill, and I sucked down my cigs. They knew who I was, and what I did on Saturday nights and had heard me on the radio. But, during the week, it didn't matter, and they didn't care. On Saturday nights though, they thought it was pretty cool when they could step onto my planet. To the credit of my family, their hearts and their doors were open to all. They were always looking for—and finding—the best in everyone, but Mom and Dad sure as hell didn't know they were packing bowls in my room.

For me, their weekday world made me timid. The only people who wanted to get near me before, were doing so for one of two major extremes: to call me ass-kicking names because I was an exile who didn't fit in and was in a band, or to grab my crotch because – I was in the band. Trust and letting people close to me was something I just didn't do, but these guys asked nothing of me except the same thing I needed from them: acceptance. And to each other, that was freely offered. We would pass the time talking mostly bullshit or walking the block, and we passed a lot of time together.

They also taught me something else vital to my life and my career: music. Now, I know that sounds crazy since I had been performing it since I was six years old, but to me, music wasn't music as they were hearing it. To my ears, it was a bass line, a melody, a phrase, a lick, and a hook. It was something to study. I heard a song in strokes. They heard the whole damn picture and they framed the bastard loud.

While none of us had a license, we had traded in our Stingray Bikes, banana seats and all, for Scott's beat-up old Malibu. I'm not sure where the brown beast came from, and the fact that nothing about it was legal was not important. What was, was that it ran and that it had a cassette player. And in that Malibu, while their stolen, burning weed and my cigarette smoke was billowing out the windows at the local gravel pit, the speakers of that old car were rattling with sounds that were of a new dimension to me. Now, I was still digging Merle, and maybe it was the contact high but, dayum! Those boys were whipping out tapes of bands called Cars, Foreigner, Fleetwood Mac, The Eagles, and the Rolling Stones. And I was grooving.

A new life, the sights, sounds, and the sentiments they sewed into my makeup gave me a new perspective on almost everything. Those boys had allowed me a vision into a new dimension that without them I would never have known. It was what most my age had already experienced. It was basic comradery and friendship, sometimes crazy but always in fun.

As much as they welcomed and even embraced me, internally, I knew I still didn't quite fit in. They were carefree and I loved and envied them for it. In fact, they thought my life was the easy one and never knew the depths of my jealousy of theirs. While having the normal teenage struggles with family dynamics and growing pains, they had something I knew I didn't, and being around them made it all the more evident to me.

Back in my world and on my safe-guarded stage, even under the influence of the red solo cup, I was still refining my chops. I would deliver our home crowd fave's: *Little Willie*, was a song that always had 'em on their feet. Or Shaun Cassidy's *That's Rock and Roll,* and Dan Seals *Bop.* I stretched my range of harmonies with Unc on *Mama Tried* and duets with Sis on a new Pam Tillis, Holly Dunn, or Cher hit of the time. Our crowd ranged from age eight to eighty and were pretty much weekend regulars, but we learned that the mood of the room could change drastically from week to week depending on weather, local events, or the phases of the moon. The band got very astute at how to read the crowd within the first five songs and from my dad's mandolin polkas to the drum rolling *Wipe Out*, we would own them for the rest of the night.

While the crowd was watching me, I would look down at my three friends out on the floor with utter envy and admiration. As crazy and as testing as life could sometimes be for them, they were comfortable there in the multitude. They possessed an internal calm. The kind of grounding that had come from always finding acceptance with their peers, by never being the last one 'not to be picked' and never having to conceal their pain or their fear on the bus. They wore a confidence that I realized I would never own, not entirely, but on stage and with the help of the Golden Ticket I had discovered in Jim's red cup, I could sure as hell make it appear like I owned the atmosphere. At least the one in this room, and sometimes, I did.

In 1979, our small town had one main road with a population that danced around six to seven hundred people. I know my mom and dad spent many worried days and nights while those boys and I piled the miles onto that ole Malibu on the backroads of town. On the radio the deejay was cranking Loverboy, Creedence, ABBA, and a woman with a husky voice and a British accent named Bonnie Tyler was blowing up our speakers with a song called *It's a Heartache*.

The national radio airplay I had received from the Ray Pennington session and the interviews I was doing over the phone, or 'phoners' were really cool at first. But now, for the first time, I was just 'one of the boys' and I was digging this new and exciting jaunt, although even then, the collision of the two and extreme worlds was a struggle for me. They talked dirt bikes, carburetors and girls. I talked mixing boards, flat versus round wound guitar strings, and chord progressions. I, of course, wanted the impossible, I wanted both worlds.

Dad knew I was losing my direction and pretty much pulled the plug on Nashville. I thought it was one of the cruelest things a man could do. I think now, it saved my life. The highway to Music City was on hold. I was cruising the backroads of town with a couple of part-time potheads and they were letting me in their circle. I'll ride the airwaves another time, or not.

I know now that such thinking or the lack of it was already under the direction of those Saturday nights and that red cup. I had begun the routine of sucking down more of the stuff from the plastic voyager before the first pick would pluck a string. The good thing, or not, was that with my family owning the largest bring your own booze dance hall in the state, was that they would bring their own booze and lots of it. Most of them carried in more of the stuff than they could ever consume and staggered out leaving many full bottles and cans on the tables. This became quite intriguing for the family clean-up crew come Sunday morning, and I had discovered yet another perk of being a part of the family and the clean-up crew. I could horde enough stash to keep a Saturday night buzz on every time the sun went down. This also, of course, made me especially popular with my weekday buds and made my status in the club shine a bit brighter.

My younger brother, Allan, as well as Sis, had developed great and lasting networks of school relationships that had sustained them, and Allan no doubt was often bewildered by his older brother. We were and remain close, yet disconnected. While younger than me, I would often yearn for his ability to fit in. He never had an interest in the stage; he had no fascination with music or felt a need to escape in it.

I wore out many pairs of shoes trying to chase normal, the kind of life my younger brother shined in so well. But my shoes were worn by feet attached to the weary soul of a country singer, and one whose life was going way off key.

Sadly, and as you know, somewhere among the branches of every family tree, you find a stem or two of addiction, and while my mom, dad, and even my grandparents never took a drink, somehow the genes that I was born with began to wear me, and they wore me tight and for too long. I knew my mom and dad were concerned and at a loss as to how to restore their child and his direction.

Songwriting, however, never stopped for me and was an involuntary action. Titles, hooks, and lyrics would come without effort on my part. My job was to know them when they came and to capture them. I have walked out of stores a thief because I would grab a box of anything off the shelf that I could use as a base to write on while following Sis around, and forget I had it. I wrote many songs that ended up on my Atlantic album during that insane time period. *10,000 Tears Ago, Where Forever Ends, More of That*, all pretty much written in the fog. A project song I am most proud of, *God Bless the Children*, was written while my body was in a chair, and my mind floating in the land of anywhere else. I had also built my home studio and was learning my way around all those knobs that I had seen at the mixing board at Hilltop studios. This would later have a major effect on all of my future records and sound.

I had developed a problem and privately, I knew it. I wasn't living life, I was just passing through and with blurred vision. It was that word that I had heard of and I had heard it many times. I was an alcoholic, addicted to the journey, to where? To anywhere away from 'me.' Alcohol was my vehicle of choice, but by this time if the well went dry, I had also cultivated more than a casual relationship with weed. Of course, helping to power my ride were the crowds at my feet by the stage. As a means to call the lead singer their bud they would be more than liberal with their loot. I had built up quite a following of these 'buds' but could tell you the names of very few.

The stage atmosphere had changed, and the fault was mine. Sis was doing her best to hide from both the crowd and from Dad just how far I was straying off the cues, off the notes, and off his map of high hopes. Unc would hug the mixing board so he could quickly mute my mic should I say something between songs that they didn't want equalized, compressed, and amplified with reverb.

I try to have no regrets except for where others were affected by my actions. I had never dreamed that I would be one who would struggle with addiction, but it knows no prejudices or biases. While many of us have had our dances with the devil, I had to hang around hell long enough to see if the bastard has a cellar. He does, I furnished the place.

Adults don't always just make children, sometimes children make adults. In April of 1992, I was about to go to the airport to pick up my first son. I was about to become a dad. Heaven was heading my way on an airplane and he was bringing a heart full of new music with him and his lyrics did not include a daddy on a bar stool. It was time for a whole new song.

Chapter 15

New Strings on an Old Guitar

In 1992, not a single note had ever been played on the song Turbo Twang. It, like much of my life, and yours, was yet to be written. But also, like all of us, the pen, to a large degree must be guided by ourselves. And mine had lost its way. It was time to start on a new page.

I really don't give a damn about shoes. Sis would always say, "You can't go on stage wearing those," and drag me to get a new pair. But there I was, sitting at a long row of tables, peaking underneath at all the pairs of shoes. I didn't look into any of the faces of anyone attached to them as they faced me. I just, all of a sudden, had an uncanny interest in footwear.

The blue Nike's had some good things to say and so did the lady in the white sandals. The guy in the shitkickers was wise and must have been a painter due to the many, various colors that graced the old leather. Then I looked down at my own pair of boots. I could not believe that they were attached to the feet that were directed by the legs which were connected to the ass that was committed to the chair—at an AA meeting. I was no longer a country singer, but an imitation thereof: a sad old country song on a Wurlitzer jukebox.

While my boots entered the room with one pair of feet, they were carrying three different and staggering entities. The mind, body, and spirit that combined, made me, and what little they understood of each other, did not get along.

Somewhere, back at my house, I still had my first guitar, the one I had been so excited about when my mom saved me from school to go pick it up from that old Sears and Roebuck store. With worn out strings, it leaned there, un-played, for years, standing in a corner with the tedious dust of life clinging to every fret. Built by its maker, it was designed to perform, of course, but there it sat, un-resonating of the music and the life it was built for. It and I had spent so much time together; we wrote, we learned songs of teenage crushes and mournful melodies of heartache. Together, we had been through a lot in the confines of my room, and with nothing but the furniture as our audience, we shined. And now, all these years later, that guitar and I were the same. No music in our souls, not a note to cling to. It was time for new strings on both of us. Now, the ambiances of fatherhood were awakening the old vibrations of life that once had echoed in my dreams, my hopes and my plans.

I had drunk as I liked to spend most of my life: alone. And usually, my habit would beckon at night, and now that Kyle had made me a father, I had noticed that on too many nights after committing to myself that I wouldn't, I would miss his bedtime rituals as I faded off into my void. I had learned how to use the golden liquids to turn off, to keep my anxieties, concerns or fears, and all emotions, on a flatline. Of course, doctors call flat line'n 'dead'.

The morning had its own ritual. I would sit at the kitchen table and drink at least three cups of coffee with the giggling sounds of my son in his small baby seat. As the sun would rise and hit the midway point of its daily route, it would bounce off the kitchen wall behind me. The big clock that hung there on that wall would reflect down onto my son's favorite and always present 'blankie' as it covered his tiny body. I would watch him as the reflection of the minute hand would do its tick-tock journey around and around and mark the beginning of his dance with time and remind me of how much of it had passed. In my mind, I would reach for that second hand on his blankie and try to turn back the time. An imaginary attempt to give us back the night before so we could do the dance one more time, not as a father and his boy, but as dad and his son. The sun, and my son, were both waking me up to a new day.

At my first twelve-step meeting, I learned quickly that my clock wasn't the only one that seemed to have malfunctioned and skipped days, months, or years. Those who belonged to all those shoes would share their stories. They did so with brutal honesty, exposing their own pain and the suffering they had bestowed on others. They spoke of regret and of shame, but more importantly, of hope and healing. Two thoughts did cross my mind. One, I really could use a drink, and two, there's a damn good song or two in this place.

But the light in the room was coming from more than just the fluorescent bulbs in the ceiling. It was emitting from the glow of those who had been in the dark for too long and had found their way back to what they now could see was what people called 'life.' They were glad to be living it and were inviting me to the party.

Sure, they knew who I was, but in there, they were shining brighter than I ever did, no matter how many lights had been aimed down at center stage. When it came to the common battle, no matter how diverse the number of attendees, we were all different, the same. We had found a room where we belonged. We had found the elusive damned normal, or at least our version of it.

I called yet another family meeting. Some of them knew that I had been caught in the vice of addiction. Others had no clue. The Saturday gigs at Warner's were at their peak and my nameless pals would keep my dependence from being thirsty.

I would need my family's support as well as time off from the band to focus on getting back in control and beginning my journey into dadhood and whatever would follow from there. This would mark the first time since I had been six years old that a Saturday night wouldn't find me on a stage in front of a drum riser. The family and the band as always, stood tall and could, and would, go on without WW until I was ready to return.

From my house, I could see the cars line up to enter the dance hall parking lot. I could hear the sounds of weekend hootin' and hollerin' and the kick drum rattling the roof. By this time, new drummer Dave Allen had taken over on drums and Unc's son and my cousin, Stephen, had joined the stage and they were turning it on.

While the band was but feet away and for the first time playing without me, I was on my living room floor with my son watching videos of Elmo. The fog in my mind beginning to clear, I would contemplate the challenging world that awaited my little man, it's many rewards and cele-brations, its wonders and its countless perils. As I held his tiny hands, my mind would wonder what, in time, would they hold? Would they wield the tools of healing, or would they clutch a weapon? Would his fingers point to the skies and lift souls, or be callused by a builder's trowel? What would his life's song be? A slow and easy ballad, or hard rock defiance? And, the question we all start asking at some point, how long would I be around to hear it? I knew these concerns were not the ones that a father would pose, but on another Saturday night many years ago, while my dad played in the band, he became the father of this son. Now, as he played for me on these Saturday nights, he was becoming the father of a dad.

After about a month away from the stage, I felt ready to return and exercised some strict adherence to plans made in advance. I would not leave my house until the crowd was in the door, the instruments were tuned, and the band in place. I would kiss my son goodnight and with my bottled water, walk across the dark field, and enter a side exit door and head directly to the mic.

I would find the notes and hit the marks, but something was different and very much so. While I had spent most of my life on the platform, I felt totally out of place and self-conscious to the extreme. I leaned more on Sis and Unc, but I felt like I had never stood on stage before. It was also the first time I ever noticed I wasn't alone behind my microphone. It was the introduction to the inner voices singing off key and in my ears. This was something totally new to me and would surely go away?

The weekdays were easier. I laid low, leaving the sanctuary of my house only to attend my weekly meetings while spending my days with my son and writing. I was very concerned that my ability to be creative would somehow be altered. I would dig out the old trusted little cassette recorder and listen back to song ideas. I was stunned at how I found many of my ideas on the tapes garbled and incoherent. Apparently, some of these inspirations hit me long after the booze did, but whatever they were, they too were to be forever lost in the broken clock.

The stars, not the singers that I had worked with, but the real ones in the sky from my front porch, looked brighter than I recalled. It was like I was seeing them for the first time. I was taking them in with the same wonder as my son did. They had disappeared for me, along with a lot of things at the bottom of that red solo cup. But during the weekdays, with the support of my family, meetings and 'daddyhood,' my new-found sober living, while challenging, was one day at a time sustainable and rewarding.

The stage however, remained my biggest challenge. It had always been a refuge, my comfort zone. Now it was anything but. I dreaded the thought of the weekend to come. Now, I had to draw from the depths of every cell, all that I had learned from my dad, Unc, and those in the band and really had to do my best at 'performing' and for me it was exhausting. There was not an ounce of exuberance in a single beat or a single chord. For the first time in my years of stage experience, I was self-conscious to the core. I was scared and with every slap of the snare, I wanted to be anywhere else. As I would find my notes to the cover song of the day, I would vaguely recognize the faces in the crowd. Some, who had taken a young boy lead singer to places during the quick intermission interludes that adolescent minds and bodies should not have been. And now here I was, an exhibition for them, serenading them, I would just hit the notes and get through the song.

Now, knowing the extreme of paranoia, I don't know how I did it, but the family, knowing what little I would share with them, did all they could to get me through the nights. I began to close off, pull my mic back further from the edge of the stage. I asked for a remodel of the dance hall so there was no seating next to or behind the band and no one asked questions when I asked to always have an escort to the restrooms. I thought it strange how people would talk about me as the singer who didn't fit in off the stage, when I was getting a strange view of people from on it. This would also later cause me to become extremely protective of my sons. Behind the mic, I would watch Sis and Unc and I would hit my marks, and I would find that smile. But on the inside, the voices of the past would join me in song. While they would only whisper, their lying chorus of doubt and of shame, would over-ride the intense volume of my band and would make my night at Warner's Dance Hall Hell. Yes, I learned to perform, but this would also be the establishment of my thoughts that my old and dear friend music had been a form of betrayal. Yet, I found a way. The intensity of the spotlight became my new ferry of escape. I would listen for the beat, and while it made me appear all the brighter, in my mind, I would grab the audio and ride the white glow to a place that would make my surroundings totally dissolve, I would sing my song and stare directly into the light.

It was during this time that late one night, Sis found me in my studio. She said it was time to get back to work. She was trying to get me back into the life I had once known and said she was booking a flight and a session back in Nashville and to have songs ready.

I did have songs ready, but I wasn't sure if I was. Sis, however, could always launch quite an aggressive campaign. When we arrived in Music City and headed to the studio, I was stunned. Knowing my apprehension, Sis drove straight to the parking lot of Hilltop Studios, the place I had made my first record at sixteen years old. It hadn't changed a bit. Being back in a recording session and in the confines of a studio, I felt my love for music and would once again begin to find a beat.

One of the songs slated for the session was one that I co-wrote with fellow Vermont artist and friend, Jamie Lee Thurston. The song, Something Bout' You, became a rapid return back to the world of Nashville and radio, with the help of Aristo Media's Jeff Walker and great reviews in then David Ross's Music Row Magazine.

Being a dad, writing, creating, and producing new songs became a form of excitement for me. Sis would handle pretty much everything else and when I wasn't with Kyle or in the studio, with coffee in hand, I would be doing 'phoner' radio interviews at my table.

I really dove into writing and with a clearer head, it took on a fresher and more dynamic course. I found myself crafting songs a lot at the AA meetings themselves, perhaps much to the dismay of those in attendance. If something came to me, I would ask someone for a piece of paper and a pen and off I would go. One such song I'm especially proud of has kind of a Bon Jovi feel. It's called If Life Was A Prayer. In it there's a line, "If life was a prayer, tell me, what would you be, could you smile at your future's history?"

I knew the answer to the question. There wasn't much I could smile about, but I was resolved to change a lot of my future's history and I knew that being in the present would be a good place to start.

I, and all the songwriting friends I know, are often asked where a song came from, or what inspired it? I know that they come from somewhere in our experiences, but unless I'm after something specific,

I really don't know. In this timeframe, finding a new form of love in fatherhood, looking back, many of them took on that direction. As a kid, Bruce Springsteen was extremely scared of thunderstorms. He had been told that the rubber tires made a car the safest place to be. At the first sight of lightning, the youngster would run to his shelter in the driveway and hide in the safety of the automobile. On many of his albums, there are car themes that run throughout.

The weekdays were filled with creativity and moving forward, yet the stage was still complex. I couldn't understand why a place I had loved so much had become such a challenge for me. While Sis and I were starting to make periodic treks to Nashville, we were still at Warner's Dance Hall on Saturday nights. Knowing I was starting to get radio play and being back in the studios, the pressure was on to get my groove back behind the mic, and I needed it fast.

I had, over time, drank myself as empty as the bottles in the returnable bin, and learned to understand it was going to take a while to refill, to regain my sense of direction, and familiarity with life as I knew it. I was hearing about the twelve steps we were supposed to take, and it took a long time to understand that those twelve steps were not steps left or right, up or down, but inward. It was a journey that I knew I would have to begin.

Somewhere on that journey was the sound that was individual to this fish who had been tirelessly swimming against the flow. One great thing the Saturday night stage offered me was a vision into what the pulse of the current musical flow was. That first trip back to Hilltop Studios and the more to follow was where my unique sound, vocally and stylistically, began to present itself and where the musicians and I began to process it. At that time, the rules when the record button was pushed was: straight ahead, keep it simple, no frills, standard country record, next song. Screw that. I knew, being an average singer, that such an approach was not going to work for me and quite frankly, I had heard enough of it. Some of these studio cats loved getting a bit crazy and we shattered the rules. I loved it when the session was over and they would say, "Wow! This is so different." Most studio musicians at the caliber that I was blessed to work with were booked solid, from one session then onto another studio or another, all day long. They would go from mine, with the drummer heading to a McGraw session, and the Bass player heading to a Chesney's. That's what they did, and they did it well. So, you knew you had something good when they would hang to listen to the rough mixes until the very last second. Kudos to the fish that swim upstream. It was nice to have some company.

I seldom go back and listen to those old records, and to hear them now, they don't sound special and to me; they're dated. But, when we counted 'em down the day the notes first saw tape, they were ahead of their time. For that, I will always be glad I grew up in front of the Missisquoi River.

I have heard a lot about some of the things I had done while under the direction of my disease, some of it I own and have made my amends wherever possible, with the realization that it will be a lifelong quest. Many of the stories I have heard about myself from those days sound damned interesting and like they would have been a lot of fun but are either absolute fiction or have been greatly exaggerated.

With the fog lifted, I was singing with my dad's band at Warner's and rocking the crowd with Dwight's Honky Tonk Man and singing harmony with Sis on Faith Hill's, Let's Go To Vegas, not having a clue that we would soon be sharing space with both of these singers on a couch in a town twelve hundred miles away.

Band: Mark Fortin, Wayne, Rylan Fowler, Scott Fowler, Unc, Soundman, and Mark Chrisawn.

Buzzy's: where it all began.

CMA Fest.

GAC with Nan.

ALL- STAR CHOIR INCLUDES: Photo Provided By: Barry McCloud Photography
Jamie Lee Thurston, Trevor Brunton, Tim Brunton, Terry Joe / Desert Heat,Ron Kingery, Scott Whitehead / Hometown
News, Kelsey, Lila McCann, Laurelyn Carter, Wayne Warner, Louis Nunnley, Ray Walker / Jordanaires, Elsa Nine, Sonja
Williams / Redd Hot Mamas, Ken Isham, Barbie Isham / Texana, Richard Young / Kentucky Headhunters,Memarie,
Brittany Roe, Kevin Sharp, Kalisa Ewing, Taylor Swift, Deborah Allen, Jason Grainger, Mila Mason, Jett Williams, Mark
McGuinn, Billy Yates, Jimmy Fortune / Statlers.

God Bless the Children Choir.

Jimmy Fortune, Wayne, Linda Davis, Jason Grainger, and John Berry.

Wayne.

Performing at the CMA Fest.

Recording.

Singing to the boys in the God Bless The Children video.

Somewhere.

Studio with Ace Lutz.

Wayne.

Warner's Dance Hall.

Wayne.

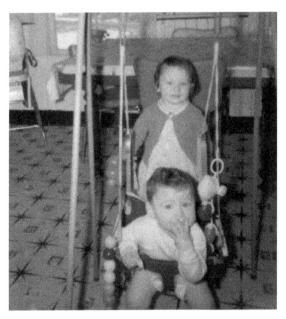

Wayne and Juanita: the making of a team.

Wayne and Juanita.

Wayne and Sis, on the bus.

Wayne, Mila Mason, Kevin Sharp, Bryan White, and Mark Collie.

Wayne's Bus.

Wayne's room in the back of the bus.

With fans, on the bus.

Chapter 16

Being Venturous

After the deal with Atlantic, I was growing tired of the music business and the bullsh*t that surrounded it. I reverted deeply into my role as dad and as always, just being one invigorated me to the core. I was weary and I was losing my passion for what had taken me so far: music. I needed to be home, with my neighbors, my people. I needed to get grounded and finally be allowed the time to process all that had unfolded. I knew a melody would come back to me and my life at some point, but right now, the chords of my life were playing something unfamiliar. They were playing a song with no structure, no verse, no chorus and it sure as hell had no clear end. It was the first time in my life that without my love for my music—any music—I had no direction.

I had done what I had committed not to, I had become 'what I do,' and without it, I had no rhythm, no reason, and no rhyme, no 'me.' I made a promise to never allow that to happen again if I ever could get me back, whoever 'me' was.

I did know who my 'me' was when the boys had a basketball or a baseball game. I was the loudest and proudest damn dad on the bench that's who 'me' was. While I had heard the roar of crowds across the country at one of our shows, it didn't come close to the round of hand claps and cheers from locals when our home teams scored. I knew from then on, the only games that were going to be involved in my life involved a board, a field, or a court and with my sons. As far as my work was concerned, the games were over.

At this point, I was thrilled to just be able to tuck my sons in at night. In them, I did find inspiration again for music. To me, love makes a vibration in the soul. With them, I felt the beat, and sometimes an idea would flow. But I was going to take some time.

Soon, I realized that I had moved my home studio around so I could watch the boys playing ball outside from my mixing board. I also noticed that I was spending more time behind it. I needed to rebuild my faith, my faith in music and in some sort of model where I could fit and without compromise. I also needed to regain my stride with what had been a lifetime of kicks to an already limping ego.

Writing was something that I knew would have to be done and it would sustain me. I could do so from home and as there had been much fighting over my songs, it was one thing I felt confident in. My song catalogue had been kept pretty much under wraps by different people along the way, with a lot of wrangling going on for many of my titles, each song sliced into different ownership percentages. I really didn't know how many words to each of my songs I even owned anymore, still don't to some, and I dug hard for every rhyme. While none of my songs were being pitched to other artists, some did find their way to their ears and requests were made and turned down by these various percentage owners. Mostly because of my talks with the multitude of labels and plans to have WW put them out. Oh, okay. I'll admit that I found it both an honor and a mystery to me why my music garnered interest from a diverse range of artists, from Brooks and Dunn to Meat Loaf.

I didn't always know the inspiration behind every song, but it was always important to me to leave them open-ended enough to make them universal, so that anyone could make the song their own. If it was love lost, to the listener, it could have been about the loss of the love of their life, whether that be a child, parent, or family pet. I also tried to make them gender neutral, so anyone could sing them. I liked and borrowed from many genres of music, but I was country based and that's what my songs reflected. I was drawn to it because to me, country music is America's soundtrack. It tells of the human experience. It can make you laugh or cry and can make you travel in time with just a few notes of a melody from the past.

I was also bootlegging from the songs I heard from my dad's old band at Buzzy's. Three chords and three minutes. As such, my approach to songwriting was a simple one, Grab 'em, bring 'em the story with a hook, and leave 'em. But 'leave 'em' wanting more – right?

While my learning—relative to classrooms—had been limited, my Uncle Arlon, Uncle Lorin, and former singer in the band, Aunt Priscilla, had been to college. Their way of being able to string a phrase always blew my mind. Their father, my sweet grampa, had also spent some time as a Vermont legislator and I would marvel at the way the graduates would help him to draft a campaign letter or a press release. I became a fan of the power of words by how the ribbons on their typewriters were being directed by their minds. Words, and my desire to create my own style as well as plant seeds in the thoughts of others, became an obsession when I would be excavating for just that right line.

Sometimes, I would challenge myself and try to put a listener in a setting. One of my favorite examples of this is demo singer Trisha Yearwood's breakout song, *She's in Love With The Boy*. Writer Jon Imes would put you in the scene, "Katie's sitt'n on the old front porch, watching the chickens peck the ground" and then goes on to explain Tommy's Truck "splash'n through the mud and the muck." I think he used four chords or so, but he put you in this love song like a movie scene.

Damn, that's writing. On a few songs, I attempted it and came close, one made it on what I still call the sunken Atlantic album: *Life After You*. "Alone at a table for two, twin champagne glasses, two menus. Eyes of confusion stare at the view, as I pull out a chair for the memory of you." I was proud to have it at least paint some kind of snapshot warranting it good enough to make the album.

People outside of the immediate town were getting used to seeing a bit more of me in those days, although except for my son's ballgames or going out to hear my dad's band play on occasion. I was and always have been a laying low type of guy.

I did, and still do, walk around our town block after dark. The route takes me by the site of where my former grade school used to stand. While the old white building has been a long time gone, the landscape is unchanged and there, in the distance, where the weeds are sprouting through the cracks in the pavement and if you know where to look, you can see what remains of an old basketball court. Sometimes, on those shadowy nights, I would find myself standing there. My memory had a clear vision, and after all I had been through, after all the miles I had been from the place, after all the successes, I would listen for the voices. They always said, "Hello."

And we all have 'em, don't we? The chorus of remembrances; the good, the bad, the fun, the sad, and while the voices seem legion, it ultimately boils down to one: the conversation our mind keeps having with itself and its overall perception of what all those voices have developed ... into you.

The voices that spoke to me weren't all bad, but like their generator, they were strong and opinionated and, of course, exaggerated. For the most part, they had been what fueled my fire.

Speakers ..., speakers were, for me, the only way to shut the bastards up. When I heard my voice blasting out of those cones with a hook and a beat that was undeniable they couldn't argue, or surely not louder than the Tannoy NFM 8s in my studio.

Being home with my sons, writing, and being in the home studio recharged me. I was feeling that it was time to get back to work on some level and I knew that Sis needed to. Performing live was something I would still resist, but without a drum keeping the beat to one of my songs, my heart was out of time.

Along with the prestige of having been on a major, Sis and I, as well as the family team, had witnessed the exhibitions that occur behind the solid gold curtains of the industry. One thing driven home was that when you hear your friends talk about how great a song must be because it's doing so well on the charts, doesn't mean sh*t. Actually, it's bullsh*t pegging red. Those major slots in the top realms of the so-called charts are almost always there due to deals made and understood in the dark, period. I don't care if it's promising radio interviews with one of their better-known artists in trade for one of the new ones that the label is trying to break, or someone in the promo department sending them weed in the mail. Spins per week, or how many times the song gets played, is what provides the data from all the reporting stations that dictate the song's position on the weekly chart.

One night in Colorado, the 'game' became such a reality for Sis and me when we were having a late dinner with a radio program director after an interview, and they were struck with panic. Realizing they had not met their promised quota of spins that week for a new major artist's song, they ran out the door and waited 'til not long before midnight to allow the song to play five times in a row to complete their end of the 'deal' before the charts came in. That deejay, while a fan of the artist, hated the song.

That is how it works; welcome to the music business. And of course, you may already have wondered many times why that song sitting in the coveted number one slot for a few weeks too long just plain … sucks Now you know. To be fair, most deejays and program directors are no happier about these 'deals' then we are, but that's just how the machines get 'greased.'

But, as I said earlier, there are those amazing people in radio who are still in it for the music. Those are the guys and gals who keep the format fresh, who help to make the discoveries that we all will be singing along to. Those who will take a chance with unknowns if the song is good and to hell with whatever label is stamped on it.

It was time to resurrect our label. It was time for B-Venturous Records to live up to its name. I, of course, had concerns. I had battle scars; the fighting to retain song publishing; paying to regain ownership of my own name; and trying to stay true to what little I knew of myself; the sound that I had developed; while rolling dice with labels. None of these tribulations did anything to curb those damned old voices in my head. No matter how much I tried to bury my head in the pillow at night, they would find an open ear for their thundering loud whisperings of doubt, of fear, of discouragement. Ah, the gift –and the curse, of artistry.

Once again, the family meetings were called, and once more, my mom made sandwiches. Assessments were made, challenges noted, and accomplishments celebrated. We would do as we had always done: pick up the pieces and go for it. And luckily for us, we had some good pieces. We had some name recognition, radio support, and, inspired by my sons, songs ready to redline in the studio. Sis had her many contacts and friends and I, while wounded, knew how to and would, turn it on when needed.

Some of my former works were still getting great reviews and we had a lot to build upon. With our family's drive and financing, along with Ray Pronto's brilliant sense of enterprise, we were ready to crank the speakers to eleven. With Aunt Priscilla and Uncle Arlon doing the accounting and Dad, Unc, Lisa, and Charlie at the wheel, B Venturous Records was about to start getting 'Venturous.'

Another one of the initial assets we had at being venturous was that the radio touring we had done nationwide had gained us great insight from program directors who were also prone to swimming against the current; many of the champions who weren't just the fictional chart chasers. There was one particular gent who I knew I needed to talk to before we initiated our plans at independence and vied for space on the board, defying the corruption that owned it.

Mike Thomas, at KFAV in Warrenton Missouri, had become a huge supporter of WW. The kind I liked. He told me when he loved a new track of mine, or when he thought I could do better. He became someone I leaned on a lot when it came to the world of radio as well as a friend and a confidante. He had been aware, both through the media as well as our own conversations, what had been taking place with regard to the up and down rhythms of WW both personally and artistically. His counsel would carry much weight for me on both fronts. He told me something that I had heard once before, that had come from the kind soul of another wise man I had reached out to by phone. Mike Thomas at KFAV said, "Sing Mr. Warner, Sing."

Once again, Sis beckoned the old studio gang. This time the session was going to take place on the outskirts of Nashville at Paul Scholten's County Q studio with engineer T.W Cargile. I had worked with T.W before, and he always knew what we were chasing, and we chased it hard. With Troy Lancaster back on guitar and co-production, Dave Pomeroy on bass, and John Gardner on drums, we laid down the basic grooves to *A Flight Called You, Surrender, Doing Something Right*, and others that I had written during my downtime.

It was great to catch up with the guys in the studio. John had been behind the kick drum on tour with the Dixie Chicks on that ominous night that literally ended their colossal career with lead singer Natalie Maine's political statement. Between takes, T.W would crank up some tracks that he was working on for a new guy named Jamie Johnson. I had done much of the pre-production at home so the session would go smoothly, and my songs would catch their groove from the countdown.

One of the challenges for me was to always get the guys to let me strip the ballads down, to let the songs breath, allow the lyrics to carry the track. I never did get them down to the bones of the song where I really wanted them at the time, but now I'm hearing new artists and new productions on the radio and it's starting to happen.

It was early in 2004 at a recording studio in Nashville, it had been a long week of meetings, but the studio time was rejuvenating. I spent hours behind the mic and behind the mixing board, and after the final session, I couldn't wait to slip out the back door for my nicotine fix.

As it turned out, I had one more track to sing, and within days a song called *Turbo Twang* would be hitting the turntable at a radio station in Pittsburgh, PA.

Chapter 17

Twang'n

The song *Turbo Twang* caught on fire and lit up request lines around the country. With Frank Bell's station leading the way, the song spread from radio tower to radio tower and was being cranked in car stereos from five-lane highways to the backwoods logging roads. Sis was inundated for interviews with WW and we tried to keep up.

While a great problem to have, the rapid reaction of an unplanned and unprepared release left us at the B-Venturous label scrambling and overwhelmed. We didn't have a completed album ready or even a follow-up single for release to keep the momentum in flow. Caught by surprise, we hadn't yet obtained nationwide distribution, a publicity firm and had no artwork for an album in motion. These issues would need to be addressed and in an expedited fashion if we were going to be able to capitalize on the staggering reaction to the song and allow the label, our label, to maximize the potential that was now being offered.

Another revelation was that the song exploded at the dance clubs and the *Turbo Twang* bass notes were blasting the subwoofers worldwide. Dancers were scuffing their heels and slappin' their knees from sea to shining sea to an off-the-cuff song written to pay wise-ass homage to a magazine critic. I was twangin' and Big & Rich were ridin' horses and saving cowboys right up the dance club charts. I didn't even know such charts existed, but they do, and we rode 'em to the top. This was especially ironic as since I had grown up on stage, I never hit the dance floor, and the closest I ever came to dancing was when my boots would lose their grip on the Vermont ice. At which point I promise you, I would do some moves that would rival Fred Astaire.

I was of course, thrilled that people were digging a song that we at B-Venturous had put out, and excited for the opportunities it could bring to the label, but inwardly, I was also very concerned. I was rapidly growing a nationwide fanbase, but they were connecting me to a song, sound, style, and subject matter that I knew was not an overall representation of who I was, as a core artist and what's more, my personal affection for the song hadn't grown one bit.

Sis and I were now in the midst of Nashville's 'in crowd.' Being welcomed under the umbrella of mother country music is an amazing sight, and the inside view is something I wish all could experience. The comradery and the family-like atmosphere among the artists is something to witness, much less be a part of. Whether its Reba quickly grabbing Dolly to adjust an earring before she jotted out on stage at the Opry, or one artist being willing to sing with another for a new single, the hang time with these people is something I will always be grateful for. It was refreshing to be able to experience this element of the business where music, people, and love really do rule. I hear that other genres are the same and from what I've experienced, I believe it to be true.

With the challenges on the label to meet the demands, along with making fatherhood my primary success in life, the pressure was intense. The traveling was extensive and we were trading our days and nights with our kids, as well as meeting and hanging out with country legends and sharing make-up chairs with other newcomers of the day. It was a constant collision of two massively different worlds and all in a blur of chaos. We rushed in and out and into and out of the next. At one of these 'ins,' Sis and I did pause long enough to hand the phone to Porter Wagoner so he could say hello to our mom; one of his biggest fans. He was glad to oblige. Wow! As I watched that man speak so kindly to my mom, my mind went back to all those years ago when his voice on that vinyl would fill the house as she decorated for whatever holiday was around the corner.

As an artist, being among this cast of people, I was amazed at how I did feel like I belonged. There was an unspoken but loudly understood awareness that we had all, at one time, been the lone fish. But in the backstage halls, the dressing rooms, the green rooms, the acceptance and encouragement of one another was astounding.

The insanity of it was invigorating to us all as a family at B-Venturous Records. Challenges were nothing new to this crew, but this one was nationwide, and we dug in. While much of the album was written, I tried to pen one that would also be a good follow-up to what was more in line with *Turbo Twang* but would also begin to hint at the WW sound that would follow. *Things You Make My Heart Say*, I thought, was a bit more crafty as far as wordplay and would also be backed by a beat that would rattle a dancefloor.

Sis would work insane hours to put together radio tours and the scheduling had to be precise. I loved meeting these strong-willed radio guys and gals and was humbled by them to the depths of my soul. As exhausting as the trips were, they were also invigorating and Sis and I would adapt to the driver calling back to us; 'ETA, 15 minutes.'

I initially fought the idea of getting a tour bus. For me, it was a defining moment of the no-turning-back point, and about 14 tons of frigg'n "real." Success, however, was helping to draw our map now, and we had a lot of map that needed to be covered. Metallic silver, the bus was long, wide, and designed for maximum comfort. Even with ten of us on it, the thing was still unbelievably roomy. With its roped mirrored ceilings and cozy stretched couches, it was laid out for multi-purposed weekly or monthly jaunts. With its dense cushioned chairs, satellite televisions and sound systems designed specifically for traveling musicians, entertainment was never in short supply.

Entering in the front galley, the full kitchen was lined with lots of seating, a large-screen television, and a table where many meetings, interviews, and for me, solo songwriting sessions would take place, it was the busiest section of the home on wheels. It extended to the long hallway that housed a bathroom and a lengthy row of bunks that were built exclusively for a traveling road show. Soundproofed, and darkened for daytime rest, the berths offered quiet respite for the weary crew of pickers and grinners. At the back, and very end of the hall, was the large grey door that led to the abode that I called mine. The room truly was my home away from home. A horse-shoe couch surrounded the whole of the space and became the perfect place to sleep under a window, where a warm breeze would try to sing me to sleep. Another large television was mounted in the corner and an additional table allowed me to get more work done as we cruised on down the road. Many closets and mirrors had been installed for stage prep and specialized shades for supreme privacy. To some degree, the Prevost was one of the most important elements of the team and a key ingredient to a successful show; getting everyone to the stage rested and on time. For me, the bus became my harbor, and my room at the back, my safety zone.

With Dad, Unc, Lisa, or Charlie at the wheel, that bus would roll from state to state, station to station, deejay to deejay. With Country Music Television (CMT) or Great American Country (GAC) alternating across the big screen on the bus, Sis and I would cheer on some of the people we were getting to know as they would make their way up the video countdowns. Through the mountains and the flatlands, the corn, cotton, and oil fields and every weather pattern in existence, we saw and experienced it all. There was little time to ponder or reflect or even to celebrate the success or worry about keeping it. It was on the bus and off the bus, back on, and on to the next stop.

There were always experiences to remind us of how far we were from home. Be it the hundreds of snow-white tents that stretched for miles in the fields of Texas as NASA officials in their dark blue overalls searched for remnants of the space shuttle Columbia or being stranded in a three-day blizzard in Fort Wayne, Indiana with Blake Shelton who was snowbound with us, hampering well thought-out schedules for all involved. I had met Blake before and I liked him. His talent was kick'n with style and his wit was quick and spot on. He had a hit that was written by someone who had become a dear friend to Sis and me back at the Music Mill, Mark Sherrill. He penned a song about a dog and a prison break and the story line to the song was genius. Blake's performance of the song *Ole Red* brought it home and up the charts.

It took a lot of snow to halt those buses and I didn't like the downtime. I passed the hours with my trusty old cassette recorder and walking into the venue we had made an appearance at the night before. Golden Girls star Bea Arthur had also performed there that same night and was gathering her belongings from the dark, empty theater. At first, I was stunned by the harsh way she was treating the staff who were there trying to help her and then I re-thought my position. I'm sure the Golden Gal was a nice woman and perhaps was no happier about being stranded than the rest of us. From what I could tell, she was traveling alone, minus a sister who would guide her every move, and void of the familiarity of family by her side whenever she took the stage. I came to the realization that she had more guts than I could ever have, but, I still hoped I would always be kind.

I never liked it when showbiz people thought they were above anyone, period. It was rare to ever see it on the Row among the artists I was privileged to have hang time with. As far as I'm concerned, I just happen to sing my little songs and am fortunate enough to have some great people like what I'm putting down.

Maybe Bea had been away from home longer than us, and for Sis and me, that was getting rough. I would stare at photos of my sons until my eyes hurt, and Sis was missing her fiancé, her daughters, and her young grandson. We also were very close to our mom and the family as a whole. While Sis and I didn't talk to Allan often, our brother's dedication to his faith was always a reminder of the one for whom he had the faith in. His devotion to family would always serve to ground and inspire us.

As long as we were in the midst of the chaos and in 'show mode,' we were fine, but when the bus wasn't rolling, or we had downtime, the air in the Prevost was thick with lonesome. I can still hear so clearly the hum of the bus generator and the whining of the wheels, Sis on her phone and me on mine. Every night those cell towers would be pinging two little voices, "Dad, when are you coming home?" They had no way of knowing that my heart had never left their side.

Emailing was a crucial social network media of the day and having access to it on the bus was fantastic. I would also pass time by answering letters between stops. I always found the combination of 'fan mail' and its connection to me very odd, still do. But, I would try to answer as many as I could and autograph a pile of photos if we found ourselves on a stretch of smooth highway. I don't know why, but if I got five hundred "I love your new songs" and one "you can't sing" it's that one, the one negative, out of the hundreds of praises that I would wrangle with on the pillow at night. I think many of us no matter what we do are like that. We want to please all it seems. But, I guess I would say this also, that my larynx has taken me around the country, gotten me into limos and on private jets. It's helped to feed my family. It tells my mama I love her and says prayers with my sons at night – what more could I ask from a voice?

We would fly home for label and family meetings and what downtime we could grab every chance we got, even if it was for just a few days. I would take it in for all it was worth, and it was worth a lot. Basketball was a passion for both of my sons and even if I got home late at night, we had a routine. I would wake the boys and we would head for the car and up the hill to the school's outside basketball court. On many late warm summer nights, there was a pair of headlights shining on a couple of young boys in their pajamas going for their three-point shots until we were ready to head home for snacks. I was away a lot, but when I was home, I was all theirs and I loved every second of it. I knew that in a few days, there would be four watery eyes looking out the window as Dad loaded his briefcase on the Prevost, and like the old days, I would be trying to hide another pair of watery eyes on the bus.

Due to the growth of the song, requests for live performances from WW had been hitting Sis's cell and her email inbox. I had stalled all I could get away with, and I knew to do so any longer could impede progress of our agenda. Although the team was stretched to the max and I was already over-taxed emotionally and physically, assembling a band that would recreate my sound, fit the image, and have the right chemistry both on stage and on the bus was going to be a challenge.

Once more, the God my mama prayed to sent a smile down on us in the form of Scott Fowler. A former bass player for Martina McBride, Scott had been in the Nashville area for a while and was plugged into the local scene of road dogs. I knew he was our guy on the spot. A laid-back Wichita, Kansas boy, he was an immediate part of the team and was quickly deemed band leader. As leader, Scott and I spent a lot of time together so he could assess my personality, style, and what kind of dynamics would work well in assembling the rest of the band. Scott was aware of my sobriety, and that was a key element factored into creating the guys that would be accumulating thousands of miles together on my bus.

Scott knew also, that with the requirements of running a label, producing songs for the album, and doing interviews, that time was limited. He also learned that I—while very aware of the need–despised rehearsals. We worked out a plan that by going back into the studio and getting a mix of just a click track with a count intro and my vocals, the band could usually practice with my voice track. I would show up when the songs were learned to see how it was going and get to know the guys in the band before we took the whole deal on the road. Without the energy of real stage, I just couldn't turn 'on.' I couldn't hit the notes, the marks, or the performance – period. The band would rehearse at a local soundstage in Nashville that had several soundproof rooms where many of the artists in town would come in and prep for the road or for a television performance with their bands. As such, I would share coffee in the lobby with a bare-footed Deana Carter while her crew was tuning up for *Strawberry Wine*, visit with Sara Evans as they worked out a song for an award show performance, or especially exciting for me, talk with Emmylou Harris about the common musicians and friends that we both shared and used on our records. Emmy's purism had been a longtime influence on my career and any short visit with her was always an inspiration.

Scott had gathered the perfect blend of musicians who worked sonically as well as dynamically. There was no time to waste in hitting all the right notes as shows were lined up and they were not small-town clubs. Dates were booked with the heavy hitters of the day and we needed to be tight. One of our first performances was for country music's biggest event of the year. I was going to follow Lee Greenwood and Billy Ray Cyrus at CMA fest on the riverfront stages, Nashville, Tennessee.

Like Toby Keith, Billy Ray Cyrus and I also shared a common thread regarding our careers. However, little did I know that after singing his song *Achy Breaky Heart* over and over from the Warner's Saturday night stage back in Vermont, that I would have a tour bus parked beside his at a major event. More astounding was that on this day, Billy Ray Cyrus would be my opening act.

We were on the Riverfront Park stages at CMA Fest 2005. Formerly known as Fan Fair, the annual four-day event was one of country music's most rejoiced occasions. Music lovers from all over the world would ascend on Nashville by the thousands for a meet and greet with their favorite artists and to take in round-the-clock concerts.

I had been to the site once before on one of our family trips, back when I was pounding out those drum beats on the back of Dad's driver's seat. Seeing the stars up close and personal through my young eyes was a sight to see. To me, they appeared otherworldly. I never thought I would be back.

Now, many of these fans had traveled here to see and hear me. There were moments—fleeting moments—when you could actually stop for a second and just say, 'Wow!' Then there were sound checks; image discussions with management; the new fiddler you were praying had his parts down, as well as hitting your notes and marks. All combined with the reality that this ride and the "wow" moments would all be over as quickly as they started.

Just the day before, I had a wake-up call regarding the harsher side of the business. I had heard about an artist who was going to be performing on the hot and humid stage the day before my show. This was a huge star who I had stood in line to see, back when I had come to Fan Fair as a kid. He'd had several major hits back in the day and was in town to perform on the massive stage. Word got through to me that this musician had assembled a band, but had no bus for shelter, for changing, or for escaping the heat. What an honor it was for me when Unc left with the bus to pick up the music legend, allowing the man to use it as his own for the day. This was a guy who had once had access to more than one bus at his disposal at any time. A sad reality to the downside of showbiz. On a good note, the guy has made a comeback and is sounding better than ever.

My bus pulled up in the reserved parking along with the multitude of other buses that carried the performers for the day's line-up. The band was excited, and they were ready. From my room in the back, I could hear Lee Greenwood singing, and *God Bless the USA* echoed from the wall of speakers that would soon be sending the sound of WW out to the massive Nashville crowd. I stepped off the bus and into Nashville's humid, summer heat. I had a short visit with Billy Ray and talked about our common friend, Harold Shedd. I was surprised at how nervous Billy was and I took his full bottle of water from him and poured a little out before handing it back to him as it looked like he was going to spill some on his shirt from shaking as heavily as he was. I was more than anxious myself and had been around artists enough to know that this was the norm. I watched from the side of the stage when the *Achy Breaky* guitar riff cranked from that huge PA system, and as soon as Billy's sneakers hit that platform he was where he was born to be.

While Billy finished his set, I was back on my bus for last minute preps for my turn on the stage. The Prevost was a madhouse with excited musicians, a few press people I didn't know, and Sis who was excited and ready. This is what she lived for, what she worked for, and what she had played a huge role in achieving. I was still wondering how I had managed to fake all these people out. I knew that in a few minutes the bullied kid with messy hair and freckles on his nose was going to get out there on the stage and do what he had always done: make-believe he belonged here.

The time was near. Billy's set was almost over, and I could hear the applause of thousands with the tag of each of his songs. I did as I had always done even before I hit the stage at Warner's: I had to have just a few minutes alone. I needed to try to get the voices all together for just a minute until the speakers could do their job. It wasn't just me out there. It was my family, the work we had done, the trials, the tribulations, and the miles. On this day, while Billy sang his closing song, Mama wasn't the only one having some hang time with the God she was praying to.

Music critic, Robert K Oermann, who had been giving me rave reviews, introduced me, and Scott's work with the band paid off in high caliber. To my left and to my right, there were country music fans as far as I could see, and my face was staring back at me on screens as big as my house. I could feel the weight of the moment as every bass note vibrated the stage and up my boots and into my soul. I was very accustomed to the Warner's dance hall crowd singing the words along with me to our best versions of the top cover songs. Here, it was something different, something new. People from all corners of the world were singing with me – to my song! Yes, *Turbo Twang* got them on their feet, but for me, the hit of the day was also being able to capture them with something more 'Wayne Warner' style. There was a song I had recorded that ended up on the album that was a bit autobiographical. Live, we did a stripped-down version of it and it took the audience right where the song was meant to. *I Didn't Stand A Chance in Hell* was a tip to the hat to how love can reach down and pull you from the depths of desolation and for me, the song was a tribute to my mom and dad, or hopefully, to anyone's mom and dad.

"I turned to the bottle, as the devil led me home, cuz for every sip that passed my lips, the more of me he owned."

The standing ovation for the song passed a huge personal test for me. I wanted to know if those who liked the *Turbo Twang* side of WW could also embrace the direction that I truly wanted to head. That, and having a successful first show with the band, was my goal of the day. To do so while making myself, and every single person in attendance buy into the fact that I belonged there in the first place, would be a personal elevation in the game.

Walking off the stage and up the ramp back to the bus, people rushed the fence reaching for the *Turbo Twang*er, asking for autographs, photos, trying to reach through to shake my hand, get a high five, and even hand me gifts. I was thrilled, I was humbled, I was baffled. I was honored, and I was terrified to the core.

We had worked hard to get here, a lifetime really, and yet, that elusive place in time called 'here' was never 'there' long enough to absorb for a second. And when 'here' was 'there,' it was only in a moment when you were too tired to be anywhere else.

After weeks of tireless work with building the band and the preparations for the first performance at the CMA Fest, we were fatigued but satisfied with all that had been achieved. Following the completion of more interviews and activities surrounding the country music celebration, a quick retreat at home was needed and welcomed. For me, the bus couldn't darken the whole of my Vermont driveway fast enough. I had stopped counting how many days we had been gone, but I always had a pretty good idea how many we would be home.

The boys and I loved our hang-time, walking past the now abandoned Warner's Dance Hall to the small town's general store for a stash of chocolate bars and sodas to bring to our basketball court. Not all three-point attempts were scored, but every second stored. I wanted every moment photographed to memory. I knew they would be replayed in my memory like high-def videos on the back of my eyelids on many sleepless nights in many nameless towns as the wheels turned under my homesick heart. I would spend hours hiding post-it notes all over the house and in their clothes so for days after my bus had rolled across many state lines, they would be finding "Daddy misses you" notes in their socks, their toys, school books, pillowcases, on their ceiling, or even in their favorite movie cases. I remember asking Garth one time how he handled leaving his family so much, he told me, 'You get used to it.' I never did, hope I never do. I know he meant to explain further, but one of us was pulled in one direction or the other. There were always two boys in the kitchen window watching the bus leave the yard and a dad who missed them before we got a mile down the road.

None of us on the bus really spoke about it, but there was beginning to be a sense, I think for all of us on the team, that home was feeling more foreign to us with each visit. I'm not sure why, perhaps it was the laid-back style that had once seemed so normal to us, a way of life that had once seemed so routine, now appeared irregular. It occurred to me that all of us on board the Prevost were trying to find that middle ground where we belonged in the realm of *Turbo Twang*. As soon as we crossed the border, we were somewhere between the laid-back green mountains and the major chaos of mainstream Music City, USA, and trying to survive the rapid confrontation of both.

Before getting back on the road, we had to make a non-stop twenty-four-hour run to Nashville for a few days to get in a few rehearsals and more meetings. Additionally, we were going to be meeting up with Frank Bell and Ray Pronto who were flying in from Pittsburg. In three days, I was scheduled to be just on the outskirts of town on a soundstage to shoot a video for the song *Turbo Twang*.

The video shoot went as video shoots go and I was again surrounded by pros. For me, Frank Bell's performance and the young actors and dancers were amazing. Other than the actual filming of the video, the behind the scenes conversations about Taylor Swift excited me, I had been living and breathing WW sights and sounds and the idea of getting involved with another artist in some way would be rewarding. We had learned a lot, been through a lot and the thought of being able to help someone would be more indication that it had all been worthwhile. Internally however, I had a concern and a major one. As someone who had been on stage from such a young age, I was worried about hers. At her age, I knew that her perception of the world would be altered greatly if her eyes were matured by the visuals presented from the stage and all that would surround it. In some capacity, I had been there, and I was more than aware of the depictions that would be forever painted in her brain and perhaps, even the fingerprints left on her body. Sis and I did have a discussion about it and we were both consoled with what we felt and saw of her mom and dad. With that in mind and as time would allow, we were both excited to play whatever role we could to help this young lady be introduced to the fine world of show business. Neither Sis nor I had any doubts that she would be embraced. Of course what we didn't know was that much to their credit, Frank Bell and cousin Ray Pronto were already in talks with the husband of the woman who had been powdering my face on the set of "Turbo Twang" and soon all would learn that Scott Borchetta had an exciting young artist signed to his new financially infused label.

Meanwhile, there was twangin' to be done. With the band loaded onto the bus, we headed out to do a combined run of concerts and radio stops, when time allowed, between the gigs. Life on the road with the band never saw a slow moment. The guys lived for it. Ranging in age from Scott's young son Rylan who at fourteen and the fiddle player and the youngest on board, to my dad, who was the relief driver and the eldest. The chemistry was fantastic. When the wheels were turning, the instruments were jammin' or the videos were crankin'.

Scott and Unc were my stage go-to's and saviors. As band leader, Scott knew my every move, when I was 'on,' when I wasn't, what I would be comfortable with and what he would not allow. Unc and I could speak throughout an entire show, and never say a word. He had watched me go through puberty on stage and knew every note of my performance style, my abilities, my strengths, and more importantly, my weaknesses.

For some reason, still beyond my understanding, while the stage had once been a second home for me, it was now where I was struggling the most. It was where all my doubts and the assertions that accompanied them would join me. It was also where I needed them the least. The anxiety of doing the show and faking my way through it would leave me with an exhaustion I had never experienced. Tiredness had no ticket on the bus, and I had to fight it. We always closed the show with *Turbo Twang* then would go right into our version of Johnny Cash's *A Ring of Fire*. As the guys would play the outro and get me off the stage, I would hit the bus long enough to make a quick good night call to the boys while at the same time changing out of my sweaty clothes. This was the routine to then go out and sign autographs while the band loaded up to go do it again. I would be calling to say goodnight to my sons from a different state tomorrow.

Crowds scared the hell out of me. The disparity to that was: I loved people. Many years of being in the public had sharpened my ability to read individuals immediately, and ninety-nine percent of those people were unquestionably gracious. When I would talk to them in the autograph line, as tired as I was, I loved every minute of it. Sis would tell me many times, "Wayne, you can't visit, there are people waiting and the bus needs to roll." I knew she was right, but these people fed my soul. They motivated me. I have shaken their hands and looked them straight in the eyes across much of this land more than once. I wish the cameras could have been on my shoulders when these country music fans whom I had never met, were offering me words of encouragement, saying with the deepest sincerity how much a single word of a song or something I had mentioned during the show meant to them. They would bring homemade goodies for the band or, having read that I was a vegetarian, bring baskets of fruit to the stage to take for the road ahead, or tell Dad, Unc, or Charlie to beware of road construction and the alternate routes to take.

I learned a lot out there on the pavement, things about life and things about physics that ole lady Pudvah never taught me in school. For instance, when, for some mysterious reason, the bus comes to an abrupt halt at sixty miles per hour, a pair of feet, linked to an artist, can do a strange thing, that is to say, that they, body attached, namely mine – can go from zero to sixty miles per hour. The band's bunks and the lounge of the bus were a blur as I flew on by. At the end of my journey, while I was laying there in a country singing heap under the dashboard, I got an extremely close-up eye-balled explanation for my rapid excursion to the front of the bus. My nose was pressed against my dad's foot, which was melded to the brake pedal, and he seemed to be wondering what I was doing there! Miss Pudvah also failed to dictate from the front of the classroom, what would happen when dear ole Dad attempts to adjust the air-conditioning on our sweet ride, but instead flips the damn switch that empties the sewer tank at a high rate of speed on Interstate 40! I'm sure though, that our beloved old school ma'am would only hope the traffic behind us were country music fans.

Sis and I spent most of our time in meetings at the back of that bus. Work and lonesome always seemed to overrun us no matter what speed we were hauling.

While memory is often vaporous for me, I never will forget the first time a woman touched me and fainted in the autograph line – what? The band had a blast with that one on the bus and said the poor woman probably had merely keeled over due to heat exhaustion.

The band grew as somewhat of an extended family out there, and all of us on that bus are deeply aware of how fortunate we are to be the owners of a rare knowledge. We got to witness and be recipients of the grace and the kindness that humanity displays, and we saw it from different landscapes day after day and night after night. Those of us who are, or have been, fortunate enough to experience this, are well aware how privileged we are to be sharing space on this planet with you.

We are all hardwired to connect. This was something that, except for my sons, I would always struggle with on a deep emotional parallel, but, through music; the right atmosphere, lyrics, and melody, a performer was in fact, correlating at a level with an audience that's like "making love" in a unique way. So says Steven Tyler, anyway.

Connecting with the crowd, however, was never important to me: connecting to every one of the 'someones' in it, was. Wayne Warner never knew how to do that, and gave up trying years ago, but WW did. He did it with his songs and his delivery. He and I were in agreement on that. I always wanted the song to be the star of the performance. To me, unless it's theater or relevant to the song, then I didn't subscribe to a bunch of dancers in thongs distracting you while I jump around like a bowl of jelly sitting on the fault line when the big one hits in order to have the song make a good delivery. If it needs all that in order to sell a melody to the masses, then that baby wasn't ready to be born in the first place and should have stayed right up in there in that womb until it could cut its own damn "chords." Now, people who can do that have talent for sure, but if the song is there, you be the co-star and let it shine. Of course, this is coming from a guy who listened to his dad play those Hank songs every Saturday night. Just sayin'.

One of the first shows on the run was one that I was very apprehensive about, and the reasons were many. It was scheduled near my home. I had not been on a Vermont stage in a few years and had vowed to maintain a healthy distance between my private home life and my career. It was also very important for me that my boys and their peers were sheltered from show business. Keeping WW elusive on the home front was something I was militant about. I also had another concern. The concert was to take place at North Country Union High School. The very same one that I walked out of with my bloodied face so many years ago, promising to never return. However, I was a man now, no longer subject to the heckles and the long ride on the yellow school bus. On this day, I would have my own decked-out Prevost swanking my name on the side.

Sis thought it would be a great place to kick things off for the long and many journeys ahead and I had agreed because it was to benefit a local cause that needed support. For that, Wayne Warner and WW would call a truce and get it done.

The place was exactly the same as I had left it abruptly and bitterly so long ago. While many years, miles, and unimaginable experiences had separated the place and me, I was traveling at that moment, back in time. NCUH had the exact same smell, sights, and sounds as it did when I was sixteen, voices and all. Right now, though, the band was in place and the auditorium was crowded, the fifteen-year-old Wayne Warner had to stay on stage left. It was time for WW to step into the light.

Sis had been right; I had called it wrong, way wrong. The show felt right from the first beat to the last, and in the lounge where I had once been so tormented, people in lines were now waiting for my autograph or to say hello. These great people on the home front blew my mind. Some came out as fans, yes, but most were there as my Vermont neighbors, wishing me luck, granting all around love and support. I was absolutely overwhelmed with appreciation and with pride for the place that I called home.

As I sat and looked down to sign the photos and CDs to those in line, something extraordinary happened. Above the crowd, I heard a voice I recognized instantly, and as friendly and kind as always, "Great show, Wayne. How have you been?" She hadn't changed much, still had her smile. I left my chair so quickly and couldn't wait to give a hug to Cynthia D, and as I did, she whispered in my ear, "I never thanked you for picking up my books." You're welcome Cynthia D, you're welcome.

Chapter 18

Mountains and Valleys

From Hartford, Connecticut to Moab, Utah, that amazing crew and I were Twang'n across the flatlands, up and down the mountains, the Blue Ridge, and the Rockies. We cruised through the deserts and rolled past the wetlands.

When time allowed, Sis would research where the country dance clubs would be en route, and we would blow their minds when the huge bus pulled into their parking lots. Most of the time this would be unannounced, and it was a blast. From places like the Cadillac Ranch to the Dusty Armadillo and all around the country, WW would walk in and disrupt the place for a while and the dancers would always line up and do the *Turbo Twang* wall to wall. Sis would bring in all kinds of things that I would sign, for as long as time allowed, before we had to roll. Once again, the warmth of the line-dancing community, the deejays and club management teams would revitalize us and help to make these long trips gratifying on so many levels.

On one of those interstates, I finally viewed the final cut of the *Turbo Twang* video and it was the source of a rare dispute among our team. There was a lot of time and a huge expense doing top-end videos, and the fault was mine for not having approved it before it had already been released. It had been a crazy time when so much was going on and we were trying to not only keep up, but to stay ahead of the crescendos of our new world. My focus had been to finish up a few remaining songs to complete the album, and I would spend hours with that little cassette recorder when the wheels were whining. Frank Bell and the line-dancing cast were the best thing about the video, but the concept was something I had to strongly contest. The theme was a cool one. It depicted a song that was contagious, and it had spread like a virus throughout the land. It was a true representation, but the video, while meant to be harmless, displayed capsules and pills that would be needed to treat the 'spell.' It was artfully done, and the graphics were clever. I however, as a recovering addict (addicted to alcohol) and knowing the extreme effects addiction was having on families across the nation, had to take a stand. The video was ultimately pulled from every source and outlet we could track down. I knew that this could and would have an impact on propelling the song to its highest form of success, but to me, and with the final support of the team, it was simply the right thing to do.

The radio visits and club stops were always a fantastic time. My continued contention was when I knew we were heading for a show. I would hear that ever familiar, 'ETA: 15 minutes', and the dread that would settle in would become heavier than the weight of the Prevost. While the missing of my family was constant, it was those times when I needed my sons the most. I severely needed their assurance, their acceptance, and their love. I needed both of their hands to walk me on to whatever stage their daddy was on tonight. Instead, I always had my pre-show call. "Good luck Dad, I love you."

"Ladies and Gentlemen, please welcome, Wayne Warner." Okay WW, let's do this.

Sis and I would watch and celebrate those artists who we had gotten to know or shared dressing rooms, green rooms, or stages with, as they made their way onto the musical map and up the charts; the ones in our Music Row 'Freshman Class'. People like Joe Nichols, Dierks Bentley, Blake Shelton, Rascal Flatts, and others. Some disappeared, never to be heard from again, more victims of the know-it-alls, and others also came to the realization that the games weren't for them.

As we were traveling, I was starting to get recognized more often. When scheduling was tight, I could not leave the bus as we re-fueled or stopped for re-stocking. We made that mistake once and got blocked in for hours by very kind people who just wanted photos, which I was glad to sign, and while doing so they were on their cells calling their friends, who were there before the ink was dry to have more photos signed. It was cool, but the limited schedules and relaxed security on board would require all "Turbo Twang" and WW swag be removed from the exterior of the bus. That, was of course, fine with Wayne Warner. I didn't want to be, nor was I, one of those artists who reached a point in their career to just complain about it. There were aspects of it that I loved, and my level of gratitude never waned. I needed the people around me to keep me going, but as we all are aware, we had to be on guard for those 'ones' in the crowd. Even in places we thought were safe zones.

During this time, Sis and I were invited by a radio station manager to join him and his wife for dinner. The bus dropped us at the motel meeting spot. We would then ride with them to the restaurant. En route to the dinner, they wanted us to see their home. Sis and I sensed something strange right away. At the house, they showed us their 'Wayne Wall.' From floor to ceiling, everything WW including things I didn't even know we had. It was weird and it was eerie. It was a long dinner and we couldn't wait to get back on the bus where new procedures were discussed and put into place.

These kinds of situations, I was learning, were what was really starting to work against me. I began my career in music for the love of it because I wanted to emulate my dad and Unc, and yes, because I wanted to fit in. To fit in, not to be an obsession on someone's wall or the target of one's thrills. I began to feel as alienated on the stage, or while I was being hidden out in a hotel room, as I had back at the school playgrounds. I wanted to feel as 'one with them' while I was in the crowd.

I was growing very concerned and frustrated about the concerts and what they were doing to me. I thought I would get over it, but the bigger the shows, the more popular I became, the more the doubts and exaggerated the voices. I still felt like it just could not be real, that all who had come to see me had fallen victim to something that was truly fictitious. Such a thought process, along with the endless hours on the road, were consuming every grain of vitality I had remaining. The love for what I once wanted was dissipating with the exhaust fumes behind the bus. There was no longer time for 'the vision' except for the one directly in front of us. My family, however, had done everything they set out to do, and I was going to do all I could to follow in that tradition.

Part of that was the sound checks. For me they were intense. They were the only time when Wayne Warner AND WW would get short tempered and everyone would know it. While many rushed through them, to me, the sound checks are the most important part of the show, and the audience deserves for them to be right. The kick needed to be felt and the vocals needed to cut. I needed to count how many steps back to the drum riser and how wide the sweet spot was. With Unc ever present on my right, along with my band surrounding me, the stage was my very controlled environment and while security was staffed, I was always escorted by insecurities.

I tried to be sure that every stage had as much familiarity as possible; bus, as close to the door as feasible; everyone always in the same place; same distance apart when achievable; same line-up, and Sis in plain view. Any deterrence from this was sure to make Scott and Unc uneasy throughout the performance. They would be unnotice-ably on the ready to do one of their amazing cover tricks to get the show off without a hitch, and to majestically pull off another one of those standing ovations. I knew I had to get a handle on whatever was going on with my stage plight before it ended the career that we all had worked so hard for. I didn't know then, not sure I know now, how when everything else was absolutely coming together, on stage, I would come apart. In stark contrast, there were those moments of exhilaration, another 'wow' moment to bring you into the reality of what you had achieved. It could be just a small incident that can cast the tiniest bit of reflection and drown you in the deepest and most refreshing pools of appreciation.

We were somewhere in Ohio. The band was in the hotel getting ready for the night's show. I was alone on the bus and writing a song that I was excited about. It wasn't one of the normal writings that came easily for me. While I didn't always know what the inspiration behind a song might be, this one held a mental image for me. Again, I wanted to make it universal, but the title alone intimated me, and I knew it demanded a song worthy of it.

The title was born on yet another airplane a few weeks earlier. Sis and I were flying back to Nashville after another quick jaunt home and another heavy-hearted goodbye, to get back on the bus. I was watching the clouds pass below and missing my boys already. Every moment with them brought on a feeling of my home state's pure maple syrup running through my veins. They were already miles behind me now and all I could think about was how much they had changed my life. I reached under the seat for my briefcase, grabbed a pen and paper and scribbled the title *A Flight Called You*.

I was working on the song when I started to hear the sounds of kids outside the bus window: lots of them. The hotel parking lot bordered a soccer field and a game was about to get underway. I watched from my darkened window as the little ones in their uniforms began to arrive, and I couldn't help but think about the ones who were the subject matter of the song that was now being penned in front of me. I knew I wasn't supposed to do it, but I knew I wasn't supposed to do it while I was thinking about how to. I put on my sunglasses and a baseball cap and headed for the shaded trees of the field. All I wanted was just a few slow minutes of the feeling that 'daddyhood' would offer; just a quick break from the fast pace that was now consuming me.

I found myself next to the bench of parents and rooting like a diseased animal for both teams. I was totally lost in the moment, all anxieties about an upcoming sound check for the night's show were lost in an Ohio soccer field. I don't recall the very kind soccer mom's name, she and her young stars of the team recognized me immediately, smiled, said, 'Hello,' and winked that the secret was safe. The whole family treated me like I belonged with them, and for just a little while, I was lost in the middle of a world I had been trying to escape as a kid, and the one I was now spinning on.

I don't know where it was that I was standing in what I felt was the 'magic field of normal' for just a few moments in time, but if I ever find it on my GPS, I will be going back. I am so grateful to that soccer mom and her family for letting a tired, country-singing, homesick dad be one of them for a little while between gigs on that day. I gave her Sis's name and said there would be tickets for the family ready for them at the show that night.

Hours later, I was on the back of the bus and the group Lonestar was singing *Amazed*. It was time for WW to step into the light. When I closed the show, I glanced down to see some familiar faces and their soccer mom waving goodbye.

Between the radio stops, show dates, traveling, and trying to run the label, we were all feeling the pressure. Added to the mix was that we had to book studio time to get the rest of the album recorded and packaged. I had somehow used every spare moment on the road and had managed to finish writing what we needed to make the album; what I thought was a good representation and couldn't wait to get them executed and the project done.

Living on the road and performing was something I had to learn, with regard to its effect on the body, vocal abilities, and energy levels.

The constant breeze on the bus from opened windows or heat and air conditioning would dry out my vocal cords to the extreme. A humidifier in my room was a life-saver and keeping it filled became a nightly routine. Everyone else on the bus ate what they wanted, when they wanted, but for me, it was a strict routine.

I wasn't some ignoramus who was in denial of the fact that the way someone's face and ass looked on their album cover had a huge effect on how it reshaped the ears of the listeners and would alter the way the songs were heard. I hated it, but the reality had been a standard driven home to me over and over again, not only by all the labels I had dealt with but also by the mannequin-like dudes that I was now sharing space with most of the time in my showbiz world, that of gents, flat in belly and handsome in face. My age had been lied about so often that I really didn't know how many times I had actually circled the sun anymore, and I found the whole 'image' thing arduous.

While difficult on the road, I did make running a daily ritual, but that was as much for retaining what was left of my sanity as anything else and also because I was a smoker, it kept my breathing in check for singing. With work and tricks of the trade, Sis and I were able to maintain with the visual department as grueling as it was, but I felt that as an industry, certain image expectations had become a very unfair standard to set upon a lot of amazing sets of vocal cords that would never get to celebrate the high notes of their abilities due to this crazy paradigm.

In my sanctuary at the back of the Prevost, I had only two DVD's that would light up my flat screen. These were live performances of Emmylou Harris and Rod Stewart. Quite the musical contrast I know, but I loved them both and I knew why. They reminded me, that like them, I needed to be true to the music, to be of service to the song and to be as real as I could be in a business of make-believe. While I was preparing for every show, one of those two would be serenading me and I would like to think I brought a little of their humanity and their dedication to realism to every stage I walked on.

There was absolutely zero time for the past to be present – except of course, the one place that everything came so natural for me, the familiar. The one place where I really didn't have to think of much else and that of course, was on stage. And there, even in just a three-minute time span of a song while the audience thought I was lost in a lyric, more than the flashbulbs were in my face.

There was also the questions, "What ta hell has happened? How did I get here? What state are we in? Why are all these people screaming at me? Do I belong here?" Yes, I had literally spent a lifetime getting to this stage and on that stage, but yet, it seemed like the stage, was where all my life's stages, would turn against me. I had heard some television pundit once say about the life of rocker Kurt Cobain that most people in the entertainment field come from some form of dysfunction, but I think if that were totally true, we would all be looking for a spotlight to stare into wouldn't we?

Either way, mine was waiting. I could hear from my room in the back of the bus that Josh Turner was closing his show and his amazing baritone voice was singing, "Don't go riding on that long black train." It was time for WW to get ready for his intro.

It had been a long, but successful run, and I couldn't tell you all the towns and cities we had been to, but I remember Nags Head, North Carolina, for a few reasons. One, because we arrived the night before we had an early morning radio interview, and this would allow the rarity of sleeping on the bus without the wheels rolling beneath us. Dad had found the most amazing and secluded place on the beach to park and we were settling in. The long phone conversations Sis and I got to have with everyone at home that night was one of the best we had been able to have in a while, as we sat on a picnic table void of the bus generator and hum of the wheels.

There was a second reason I remember that stop so well. As I looked out at the sky over the ocean, I was reminded that there are some scenes that can only be painted by the imagination of a deity, where chaos can be brushed into peace. After talking to my sons and taking in that sky, peace was what I was feeling. The break offered a glance of reflection. The sounds of the waves rolling in stirred feelings of accomplishment, of jobs well done. We had traveled thousands of miles safely, done many shows successfully, and left radio stations with friends made.

Then it all changed and quickly. The winds blew up and the sky turned dark. By the time we got back to the bus, the weather channel was talking about tornados. Sis and I had been through one before on the long road to here.

I remembered it like it was yesterday. It began as a beautiful spring day in the spring of 1998. I don't recall the name of the studio, but it was damn awesome. It was right next to the great Centennial Park on Nashville's West End. Olivia Newton-John was having some work done on her tracks there while we were doing the very final overdubs on the album that was later to be my intro into the great land of major labels. We had worked on it for years and had hauled those two-inch master tapes from studio to studio and had a lot of dollars invested in them. This would be the final stage of our hard work. From the studio, we drove a few minutes to Masterfonics to pick up some copies we had asked them to duplicate for us earlier. On the way, the radio started beeping, talking about a storm.

Everyone at Masterfonics at 28 Music Square was getting quite the kick out of Sis and me as we watched their television screen. It was flashing warnings in every color Crayola ever heard of, but the folks at 28 Music Square were just laughing at us. Ah you guys from Vermont. Yeah. You have your snow, but we know our weather. There ain't never been a tornado hit Music Square or downtown Nashville. Never. Well, that may be true, but that's because it was waiting for my ass to be on Music-damn-Square or downtown Nashville Tenne-damn-see and when that thing hit, Sis and I knew we weren't going to be building a snowman.

The radio in our Mitsubishi Eclipse was blasting the emergency broadcast services and light poles were breaking off beside us as that tornado that wasn't going to frigg'n hit was hitting right behind our asses all the way to the condo. Those things will suck the air clean out of your country singing chest. The radio was blaring, *Get in the cellar, get in the cellar.* "That's great information," Sis and I were saying, "we ain't got no damn cellar, we ain't got no damn cellar!" Sis could barely breathe and was scrambling, putting blankets and pillows in the tub, looking scared to death. She was screamin', "Get in the tub, get in the tub!" Her face then changed to some sorta shape that seemed to be asking this, "What ta f**k?" When I hollered, "Get out ta' tub, get out ta' tub." She looked dazed, I said, "Get out'a the way, these frigg'n masters are going in the tub." We wrapped them in trash bags, covered them gently and waited for the howling of the storm to stop. Yah just gotta love Sis and tornados that are never gonna hit – don't ya?

Well, that tornado that wasn't going to hit, shut that city down. There was no power, no water, no streetlights, and no roof on the studio we were cutting tracks in just hours earlier. It took a few days, but as soon as the airport was cleaned up and running, Sis and I, masters in hand, were glad for an excuse to get home. We were looking ragged and scared the hell out of the first-class passengers when we took our seats, but hey, we were going home. We were going where tornados don't hit.

The wind blew hard in Nags Head, but tornadoes never did come that night. In the shelter of the Prevost, we settled in for an early morning wake-up call and another declaration of 'ETA: fifteen minutes.'

Chapter 19

God Bless the Children

"Somewhere, out there, he sits all alone
Waiting again tonight, for mommy to come home
She says she has bills to pay, and that he's only in her
Listen close, can't you hear him crying?"

– *God Bless the Children*, Wayne Warner

It was February 2006. The buses of other artists and SUV's were filling the parking lot of a discrete Nashville sound stage to shoot yet another video. Cameras and lights were things I tried to stay away from as much as possible, but this was an occasion I had been waiting for.

It had been months in the planning, scheduled, rescheduled, then scheduled again. Finally, the day was here. Making it especially profound for me was that due to the nature of the project, this would be one of the rare occasions when my sons were brought into the land of WW. Having them not only with me in Nashville, but also involved in this event, united the best of my two worlds. This would be what I would go on to call the Everest of my career.

The road had been taking its toll. While the GPS always led the bus to our exact destination, I was losing total sense of direction with regard to everything WW. After all the miles, the bullsh*t with the majors, the fights for my publishing and even my own name. I was tired. I would have kids ask me for autographs who said, "Wow, I wanna be a singer just like you." But they had something I no longer had, when they talked about their dreams; they had a light in their eyes that was no longer reflected in my mirror. They had a passion, a love for the music. It wasn't music to me anymore; it was a chart position; an opinion from a critic; a session to be booked, and a song that needed writing. It was vying to stay within excepted standards of the format; it was the trials of the stage; the dueling games with the powers that be, and the ceaseless ache of missing home and my sons. Signing photos for those kids on my tour bus who so badly wanted to be me, a part of me badly wanted to be them, if only just long enough to turn the light back on, to be able to hear the music again.

Sis could sense the situation was nearing critical. Yes, the tour buses, the perks and the recognition were all cool, but the world didn't need another 'so-so' singer. I had to make it matter or go home. I did love the fact that we were helping to give credibility to independent artists to some degree. I was well aware that there were many writers and singers out there much more talented than I, and who, by circumstance, weren't offered the rewards that I had redeemed. I wanted to play a role in changing those dynamics and in leveling the field in whatever way I could. But there had to be more. This day was my 'more.'

I think it was somewhere in Michigan that the project was conceived. After a late-night interview, I fell onto a motel bed in my jeans. Somewhere in that grey area just before sleep, I heard the familiar voice of Barbara Walters. It was a 3 am rerun of a segment she had done about adoption. She herself, the mother of an adopted daughter, the show featured several photos of children in need of homes. The pictures were powerful and had been taken professionally by an organization called the Heart Gallery. Its mission was to help unite these beautiful children with families to call their own. I sat up and wrote down the name on the motel stationary and put the piece of paper in the pocket of my jeans.

Back on the road the next day, I found the note and told Sis about the organization. Right away I could see the wheels in her head were spinning faster than those on the Prevost. After doing some research, she sat at the bus table and said she had an idea. She brought up a song title I had forgotten long ago. *God Bless the Children* was a song that was written from the heart and was from the perspective of a lost and broken child. I had no idea what prompted the song at the time, and it had been delivered to my pen in a matter of minutes. It was born long before I became a dad of adopted children, but somehow, it seemed as if it had been written in advance and specifically for this time, and for this project. The concept was to use the song with those photos from the Heart Gallery to help bring awareness to foster care and adoption.

This was the meaning that I had been looking for. It would render the platform that I had been afforded, and the time spent away from my sons, meaningful. Adoption had changed my life. I had tucked in the reasons for such on so many nights. I was energized by the idea of this project and could think of nothing else.

Sis's plan grew larger with every mile we rolled. Nashville had done very few large, united, cast projects and we talked about creating a choir of artists, as well as children, to unite for the project. We had been fortunate to have befriended many new artists that would be lighting up the radio dashboards in the future, as well as some of the legends who had already paved their way. While on the road between gigs and interviews, Sis and I began to structure the plan.

Scheduling such a massive video shoot around so many artists and their itineraries was going to be a complex mission, but we dedicated every moment we could find to the project. The first and key man on board was John Lloyd Miller. The selection of John to shoot the video was perfection in many ways. Foremost was his talent. He had been involved in many of Garth's videos, including *The Dance,* and importantly to me, he brought a passion to the project that was from the heart and soul, an element brought by few in the business with his capabilities. John, too, was the dad of two adopted children.

Several months of phone calls from the bus to friends, publicists, management teams, and artists and the choir was beginning to build. After having set and reset many dates, we finally nailed one down and began putting the rest of the many pieces together.

From what my many travels have taught me, there's a common theme of passion among our neighbors, a thread of compassion that weaves from town to town and state to state. The Nashville music community exemplified this so perfectly on the day we filmed the video. Most knew each other; some were meeting for the first time. Entering the huge room were a blend of artists whose careers were experiencing every level of success the business had to offer, from entry to renowned. Hugs were given and hands were shaken. Electricity was in the air and soon the collective passion for a common cause, blended with the gifted voices of grounded angels, would fill the room. From Jimmy Fortune of the Statler Brothers, to one of The Kentucky Headhunters, the video crew began to assemble the singers to their places on the stage.

Having the daughter of Hank Sr. as a member of the chorus was another honor. Jett Williams was born soon after the death of her famous father and discreetly put up for adoption. Somehow, she grew up feeling a connection to *I'm So Lonesome I Could Cry* and after many years and as many struggles, she found the correlation. To me, there would be no denying who she was. Her blue eyes displayed a kind of deep that could only be inherited by the writer of such profound and mournful songs, and with whom she would ultimately find she shared the blood.

They kept coming, so many familiar faces. A lot were friends, some were friends of friends. It was great to see Scott and Andrea Swift as they brought Taylor to the set. By now, Taylor's deal with Big Machine was in place and work on her first album, the one that would soon introduce her to the world, was being recorded.

I got to catch up with Taylor for a bit while Scott took Sis out to hear some of the new tracks they were working on. Taylor was excited about how things were going in the studio. Once again, the co-write that we had done had been forgotten, until seeing her brought the song back to memory. A lot of experiences had taken place for both of us since the song was written, and its origins remained vague in our memories. I quickly sang her the finished melody and completed lyrics as we were being yanked in different directions for the filming. We both liked the song, but as of that day, the co-write already forgotten in the chaos more than once, would be gone once more. *The Middle of The Light* was about to go dark – for years.

The scene was intense. Lights and cameras being set, hair and make-up people all around us, everyone catching up with one another. Finally, with all the choir in place and lights and cameras ready, John Lloyd Miller called out, "roll sound" and the place came to life. When that choir of voices sang together, it felt like it was generated by one heartbeat in time with the song, and the energy was amazing.

There they were, so many of them, singing my words: "God bless the Children, guard them and lead them, listen close, can't you hear them crying?"

Elvis Presley's famous Jordanaires stood directly behind me on the massive platform. Hearing the harmonies that had jumped off the vinyl of the king of rock and roll, singing directly into my ears – on my song, yeah, that would be one of those 'wow' moments!

I had sat behind the mixing boards with some of the best hit makers in the business, and I needed to draw on those skills now as I produced the biggest project I had ever been a part of. In capturing the voices of the choir on the record, I wanted to be sure we got the magic of the room on tape. I was now producing the legends and the mega-stars of tomorrow for a project that I believed in. It had to be right. Due to the fact we had so many professionals, it came off better than I could have ever envisioned.

After many takes from alternate angles, all of them fantastic, John Lloyd Miller called the choir segment a wrap. Next, came the part that I was of course, apprehensive about. The WW solo parts and closeups. I tried to thank every artist that devoted so much of their time to the project, as well as lending their names and their talents. They were asking for nothing but the reward of helping the cause. This universal theme in the field of music is something I will always be honored to be part of. Faith Hill had a last-minute emergency scheduling conflict that we were well aware and in full support of, and we had gone back and forth with Martina McBride and basketball Hall of Famer Magic Johnson, trying to make it work until our team finally closed the door.

In another division of the studio, the scene and the lights were set for the more intimate verses, for which much of the delivery was depending on the abilities of WW. There were so many cameras in my face, so many people involved for just shooting me. Why? I was now out of my comfort zone. On stage, I had become skillful at hiding it. I could cover the moment by atmosphere, by the thunder of the kick drum, but this was a day for closeups meant to be captured in high definition.

After several attempts of trying to get the right 'feel,' John Lloyd Miller pulled his magic and said, "Cut." He was saying something to his assistant. Two seats were brought in to the closed set and put just outside of camera range. Then he had Kyle and Keenan escorted into the room to sit in the chairs. He came to me and whispered in my ear, "Sing it to your sons." The rest was done in one take.

We took a few days off and my boys spent a few days hanging with me in Music City. This time, they would be leaving me. It wasn't any easier. When I was called to go and approve the final edit for the video of *God Bless the Children*, I was amazed at what I saw; it had come together perfectly. I was also stunned by a realization during the video playback. Something totally unplanned, yet there it was, so obvious, a plan bigger than mine had been in motion since the first drop of ink had dripped from my pen and onto the page that night so long ago when the song was born.

What was staring back at me was a lesson. When you get a nudge to take the high road, take it! There's not always a lot of traffic, not as much as there should be, and when good intentions and love are behind the wheel, let them do the driving. Anyone who has seen the video may perhaps observe also, that there in the front row of the choir, was a colossal but quiet victory. Country music's all-star choir was singing with kids of every race, from every background, making a statement to the establishment, to the nation, that it's time for a new day. It was a statement I had wanted to make for a long time but didn't know how. There it was, in massive unity, in majestic harmony. The song and video are headlined as a project for foster care and adoption awareness. For me, it is that, but also much more, and to that, I say, "Amen", to the God my mama prays to, and whatever one you do, too.

The Heart Gallery did unite with the project and provided photos for the video, just as Sis had envisioned many miles ago on the bus. We also wanted to donate the project to an organization who could help the project to be a voice for the children. It became the most successful PSA campaign for The Dave Thomas for Adoption Foundation and was advertised on every placemat at the multitude of Wendy's restaurants around the country. I received mail from people from all around the world who wanted to share photos of their 'new families' and credited the video for their new lives. This meant more to me than any gold record could. The project was the genesis for the formation of my own associated Melodical Hearts Foundation, and we have done similar projects to raise awareness for causes that need social dialogue and responsiveness. The foundation introduced yet another source of inspiration for me with what it could do to produce what I called "project songs". Productions that like "God Bless the Children," could raise awareness in a sonic way and reach ears that would otherwise be void of the message.

We knew that the song would have no significance as far as commercial radio. It had been costly and extremely time-consuming. Any pen-pusher would say such an undertaking would be a detrimental mistake and we knew we would have to work double-duty to satisfy agendas with the label. But the cause and the meaning behind it would be worth the cost on all fronts, and as importantly, the rejuvenation that it fed to the hungry soul of this artist, and in fact, the whole of the team, was a desperately needed infusion.

Chapter 20

Cracks

The massive windshield on the bus was choking on the white lines of the road and it would swallow them whole one after the other. Some of my favorite times on the road were spent sitting up front as my dad helped to keep the bus on schedule. There, as we chased the headlights and pushed the wind, talk would flow easily between the old band leader and his son. It would mark the first time I would begin to stop seeing my dad as not only a dad, but as a man. A man with a past, a one-time youth who had voices of his own, a man with fears and pain, hopes, and dreams. Growing up, he was a busy man and not one who would display emotion. I respected him to his core and my admiration for him was such that no matter how high the stage, I would ever grace, I would still feel as though I was at his feet. In my eyes, he could do little wrong. I knew he was human, and there were some afflictions of the flesh that he would unknowingly cast upon me. He grew up in a different time. What he and his family had gained in success had been earned laboriously and tirelessly. His drive for financial reward, however, had left me with a deep internal resentment for the greenback. I should have been, could have been, fiscally wealthy many times over, and it did not escape me that I would sabotage it every time. I internally debated for many miles, on many runs, if such was the issue of my stage turmoil.

This was a topic we never discussed, but we covered everything else under the sun or the moon, depending on the time of day or night, and there were many of both. My dad and I talked about how far we had come; we talked about faith, the question of God, relationships, raising children, and sometimes we just marveled that we were there, wherever 'there' was.

One night that summer of 2005, 'there' meant performing at the Talladega Superspeedway in Alabama. I was sharing the spotlight with actor Adam Sandler as he performed his duties as grand marshal for the event. Richard Petty arrived right next to my bus window on a golf cart that displayed a giant number '43' on the side of it. Sis and I thought about taking it for a spin with a certain actor while Mr. Petty was getting mobbed by autograph seekers. Sometimes, you just have to do things to entertain yourself on the road, especially when you are the entertainment. I won't say much more on the subject, except to say, them golf carts – will haul ass.

With the exception of the live concerts and missing home, the road was becoming routine. Other obligations, when time allowed, would later include accepting speech invitations that were generated from the *God Bless the Children* Video. I accepted such an invite to introduce the video for an adoption fundraising event in Scottsdale, Arizona after being contacted by PGA golfer Kirk Triplett. Getting to know Kirk is another gift that my career has awarded me. A father of adopted children himself, he has done so much for the adoption forum and far beyond what he would acknowledge. The night of the event, I made an entry into yet another world I had never circled. There were names there from every sport that bounced or rolled a ball and they had brought their wallets. Sis and I were there for the weekend and by the time we left, a lot of money had been raised for the organization and friends were made. Again, a testimony to the great hearts of people.

More speeches were made by invitations from Governors, adoption agencies, and foundations. While giving talks was naturally out of my comfort zone, the topic was something I was intensely passionate about and I would simply let my heart do the talking. I would try to do them as often as I could, while at the same time stay ahead of the immediate demands with recording and the touring.

I knew—we knew—the challenges we were up against. As an independent artist, a large shadow backed by the light of success had been cast—my own, and I was now living in it. The oddity of the achievement with *Turbo Twang* on an indie label was going to be hard to sustain, if not impossible. Not only physically for our small team, but in virtually every way. With me as the label's sole artist, the demands to write, record, do the interviews, and perform, as well as stay in shape to meet all these obligations, was something we were all ill-prepared for. Also, we were constantly combating every obstacle the majors had in place for people like us, who dared to make waves in their waters, or at least the ones that they had laid claim to, and my shadow had reached their beaches. More importantly to me, was that I would lay awake at night and watch those curtains dance with the breeze, I would stare at the pictures of my sons, and thank the God my mama prayed to that I was their dad, even while I was rolling further and further away.

The good ole USA never let us down when it came to new and amazing things to discover as we rolled on through. The darkened windows of the bus served as never-ending movie screens playing tributes to the old and to the new. To the youth, and to the ageing all of it a testimony to the earthly creations of mankind, shared only by the majestic surroundings created by the God of a higher dimension, and of our individual understanding. There were also the times when the Heavens above, and the earth below, would appear to be playing alternate songs, in different tempos. Or perhaps, not even in agreement in the types of music that should be played in the first place.

Something compelled us to pull over one time to take a walk through a modern-day town that had been completely deserted. Strolling down the desolate streets was an alarming ambience to all sensations. Toy trucks and dolls left out on the ground near rusting swing sets. Pet food dishes left empty next to dilapidated dog houses, consigned too long to the discretion of the weather patterns. Doors to houses would slam open and shut in the breeze, and former lawns had matured into small fields of wildflowers and tall weeds. I was drawn to the curb of one home in particular. The white one-story structure stood silent and still except for the curtains that were dancing through opened windows. The short-paved driveway empty except for what looked like some old bicycle parts with a clothesline off to one side. There were signs of young boyhood gatherings on the property. Just off to the left-hand corner of the house stood a rusted-out pole crowned by a basketball hoop. Tall grass had re-claimed victory over the spot where many pairs of sneakers had once worn it down to dirt, as ball handlers would battle for victory scores.

I thought about the multiple stories of life that may have taken place under that forgotten roof. I pictured Thanksgiving dinners, nervous first days of school, celebrations, and heartaches. I thought about the day they packed up and said goodbye to the place for the last time, like all their neighbors had done, and I wondered why. A little further down the street stood a wooden church. Its tall steeple overlooking what had once been the homes of its patrons. In it, were the echoes of many "I do's" and as many tear stains of last goodbye's, both happenings touched by music. Some kind soul would no doubt have been sitting on a stool guiding the organ through a jubilant *Here Comes the Bride* or the tearful *Amazing Grace*.

It was unnerving and ghostly. It was as if some forsaken disease had come through and wiped out all human existence. I guess, in some form, it had; a plague by the name of poverty. Brought on by the signs of what would become the recession of 2007. This was not the first we had seen of its malaise. With the bus parked there on the forsaken street, we walked along and took in the nature of how time deserts 'things,' and how ultimately, 'things' will desert time.

Life affects art of course, and the affliction also hit the music business, and the record labels were shivering with a high fever of surprise. The scourge however, left no consequence on new music reaching the ears of the music fans. In fact, in that respect, they were feeling better than ever.

File sharing was the pill for their zeal and it too was contagious, and especially transmittable. Free, infectious, in high quality, and right under the noses of the major labels who never saw it coming. The record giants had totally failed to adjust to, and stay ahead of, the technologies that were transforming the industry. The same day a song was released, it would bounce around every corner of the world on free filesharing sites like Napster and LimeWire. The new song-delivery approach was killing the cash registers for the labels, but hugely expanding the fan bases and exposure for artists whose grooves were being flung around from satellite to satellite and in regions of all languages. There is much debate among the artistic community about the pros and cons of having the music so readily available, shared, and easily duplicated. I sit somewhere in the middle of the deliberation. It was, however, giving us as a team, great insight into what the music fans were swapping with regard to WW's music tracks. This, for me, was especially exciting because they were swapping much more than just the *Turbo Twang* pulsation that introduced them to me. They were also digging the tracks of songs that were more of an expanded reflection of the artist Wayne Warner, making me feel much more of a worthy ambassador of the gift.

In the oceans of art, there are many and great fountains from which to drink, but my heart had to be in tune with the message, and this was a sign that I was on track. I didn't want my art to be a watered-down version of my purpose. A pyramid gets smaller as it reaches its top; I wanted to remain focused on my foundation. There are songs like *Turbo Twang* that need to be written, but others, painted instead.

Award-winning and celebrated recording artist, Eric Clapton, says in his autobiography that, "The music scene today is 95 percent rubbish, 5 percent pure." He goes on to say, that he believes that "By the end of the decade, many of the existing record companies will be gone – and will not be a great loss, but that "the music survives and will find its way to us."

While WW was always rolling further away from home and into the light, my boys didn't care much about any of the showbiz world and to me, they were my best buds. While the bond with them was somehow growing even stronger, the longtime relationship between their mother and me was distancing like the miles that had been between us. The two worlds we were now living in were different to the extremes and the relationship fell into the dark chasm of the diversity.

The more success I was having on one end meant severe deterioration at the other. Both ends were beginning to signal wear. Sis was growing concerned and frustrated. I was asking her to get me out of concert dates, to cancel interviews. She would ask me why, and I really didn't have the answer, but looking back, there was just very little of Wayne Warner or WW left to do them. There was no doubt, more layers of the famous MAC stage make-up being applied to start to fill what were the early signs of cracks in the world of WW.

Sis was also running on fumes. Night after night as the wheels turned, I would get up to find Sis working on her computer, trying to keep our work and the bus on schedule. As always, no matter how little sleep was gifted, early in the morning we would hear the famous words, 'ETA: 15 minutes.'

In an interview with Dan Rather, Norah Jones once said about the height of her career that she didn't feel that she would ever want to return to being "in the eye of that storm." Well, we weren't in the eye of the storm, but there were days where it sure felt like it was hailing in my world inside that bus. Most of the storms were internal and spawned by the mind of an artist. The adrenaline and the excessive high and for me, the exhaustion of a performance with a standing ovation with *so* many people, and just a few hours later, the total isolation of being unable to sleep at three in the morning with not a soul to talk to. I would call home every night to check in on my boys. Though the room in the back of my bus would be darkened, their little voices would be like sunshine to my ears, but just inches away, the face of an artist would rain. ETA – 15 minutes

Every show we did and every stop we made, there were singers and writers who thought WW somehow held the enchanted ticket to their dreams. Could I record one of their songs? Could I get their demo to a record label? Could I introduce them to a record producer? On the bus, we had a box in the cargo bin that became overflowing with CDs from these talented folks from across the land. And then, there were the invites: could I sing one of my songs that was 'their' song for a wedding, at a school graduation, a funeral? The most challenging were the requests to participate in fundraisers. Would WW do a benefit show for a cancer patient? For someone who had lost their home in a fire? Or, for a child that had been hurt in an accident?

The problem, is that if you look back on that paragraph, you will see a *lot* of question marks. Both WW and Wayne Warner wanted desperately to say "Yes" to every single one. I wanted to do them all, to help them all. The idea that they wanted me or one of my songs to be a part of something so astounding in their lives was monumental to me, and I will always be grateful for the invitations. To except one, though, would be impossible, made worse by the fact that if we did in fact show up at any such event, it would surely get press exposure and create hard feelings and negative press for not having shown up at the others. I also tried committing myself to the unattainable challenge of listening to every solitary CD that was passed on to me. On this, I failed also, but, I did listen to hundreds as we traveled on down the road. It really does fit under the 'damned if you do, damned if you don't' heading. But, on a personal level, I always wanted to crash one of those wedding invites or graduation parties.

The *God Bless the Children* project, and the reaction to it, rejuvenated my faith in the power of music, but did nothing to distill my contention with the stage. Constant internal investigations were starting to hint that I was just plain and simply uncomfortable with the attention of it and, to the extreme. Signing autographs was very embarrassing to me, still is. This was especially true if we were near the base of any of our armed forces. Any of these people in uniform are heroes of mine, and I do use the term literally. When they would ask me to sign something I was humbled to my soul and began a custom. I had a notebook assigned only for this purpose and when they asked me for an autograph I would say, "I'll give you mine, if you give me yours". I collected hundreds of names, and meeting those amazing people is another reward of the gig.

I don't know what highway we were on when we heard it for the first time, Sis and I recognized the voice instantly and smiled as we cranked the radio. *"When you think happiness, I hope you think that little black dress, think of my head on your chest, and my old faded jeans. And when you think Tim McGraw, I hope you think of me."*

By the time the first chorus ended, we knew that Taylor Swift had her first hit and we were *thrilled*. Sis and I sent out a quick email to Andrea and Taylor immediately and congratulated them on the song and for what was surely about to unfold.

Again, for a second, as I heard her song come over that radio, I had a whisper of concern. I knew from experience that the stage for one so young can—and would—offer a unique view of a small, but real faction of humanity for which we belong, a point of reference seen by few others. I also knew of her family dynamics. Her mom Andrea was a strong-willed and self-made independent woman who would guide with a loving and firm heart, and her dad was a playful 'shake it off' kinda man who knew how to go after it. Both had the soulful and mindful makeup to attain and retain success. With them as her guide, she would be okay. Without them, she would implode. It was only fame that would be new for Taylor. Money had always been a companion; she had grown up in a multi-million-dollar estate with a vacation home in New Jersey. Growing up in such a fashion would help her to maintain her identity and serve to keep her grounded on some level in the world she was about to enter.

Taylor, of course, had the voices of her past also. Another deep, artist-type, and misunderstood in the learning halls of Pennsylvania, she also had grown up alienated and on the receiving end of bullying's sharp tongue. She, though, used it to toughen herself and to drive her ambitions. Having originally secured a short-lived, and little known about development deal with RCA before Frank Bell and Ray Pronto set the gears of the Big Machine in motion, Taylor knew the RCA deal was not for her. The intellectual heads of RCA wanted her to do what the deal infers, 'develop,' grow up, to be able to relate to a more matured country audience.

Taylor, however, had other plans. She had the same problem I had when I made my first record in Nashville and tried to find age-appropriate songs and found it difficult. To her credit, she became an architect, she created music that hit her own generation of country fans and she nailed them right between the eyes. She did it with songs that would identify with their experiences, with their hearts, and with their souls. Millions would ultimately identify, and the connection would be reflected by the number of album sales around the world.

Taylor also had a secret weapon when it came to radio, one that few others employed. A tool that I especially, who was never handy in the kitchen, would ever own: cookies. Taylor would bake huge supplies of her homemade delights to deliver to the deejays while Andrea was driving her around on her first radio tour. I, on the other hand, can't even thaw ice – in a microwave – on a hot day.

While radio program directors were talking with their mouths full, we were still twanging and finally wrapping up the album. Being in the studio was something I never tired of. Hearing my melodies and my lyrics come to life, one guitar lick and drum roll at a time, would always narrow my world to a single set of speakers. I tried to plant a message in every song I wrote that would be heard if the heart was in the right state of mind. In the studio, the music was always my friend, but the pressure was on. We—the team, the label—needed to keep the forward thrust in motion. In my view, and mine is not a lonely tongue on the subject, the country format makes a mistake.

When the Country genre discovers their new flavor of the day, they have them cranking out songs one after the other like tokens pouring out of a slot machine. One song going down the chart, another coming up. That's cool, for a minute. However, they shove these artists down your throat until you choke on 'em. It makes it impossible for the artists to write or find good quality songs at such a rate and they get exhausted. But the labels know what they're doing, right? The next thing you know, you're burned out on the artist, the artist is burned out, and everyone is on to the next flavor. I was there during Shania's peak years; they couldn't get enough. She, like many other former kings and queens of the airwaves, now struggle to get any of their new material on the radio.

Pop artists tend to take a longer approach and the one I subscribe to. Many take years between albums, but there's an enthusiasm, there's anticipation and excitement in the pause and then, when the album does drop, it's one that was well worth the wait.

I, however, was Turbo Twang'n, and that's a lot of banjo notes away from Elton John. While on the road, Sis was starting to play some of the new tracks off the album to friends at radio. Some loved them, others said, "This don't sound like *Turbo Twang*." No Kidding! For me, as an artist, and as a part of the label, I knew this was the shadow that was going to be hard to walk out of. I also knew that I had to be true to the artist I was and I could not compromise by writing a whole album of 'Turbo Twangs.' I would stand by the album knowing it would find its audience.

Maybe it was due to the fact that like many, I grew up around name calling. Relative to my music, my own identity was crucial, and I was sensitive to being labeled. I know they thought they were being kind when people in the business would often compare me to other artists. They must have been onto something as they were often making reference to the same ones, Tom Petty goes country, the hillbilly side of Cat Stevens, or Buddy Holly, and even Meatloaf. I know these analogies were meant well, and while I had of course, heard of all these esteemed artists, I was not really familiar with many of their recordings, I made a conscious effort to avoid listening to their music for fear of mistakenly adapting more of their sonic direction.

Of course, this is show business, the grown-up's playground. As such, name calling reigns supreme. I had long dismissed my 'cosmopolitan' image that had been created and assigned to me by Atlantic records, and my inner hippy was hanging loose. I take claim for the edgier Rolling Stone Jagger look over the more country Chesney presence I once heard about, and by now, alternate quotes were being tossed around in print to describe yours truly. Some Sis would share with me; others she would not. "The messy with elegance style of the artist" wrote one author, and the words reclusive and eccentric started to share a lot of ink. I didn't know where they retrieved the 'elegance' from, but for the most part, I had to own the others. I confess, I did google 'eccentric.' I didn't love the connection, but, bottom line, I really was getting a distaste for being called anything and was beginning to feel a longing to just get the simple Wayne Warner back or, what I could remember of him. I did know he was just a simple and awkward boy from the country with messy hair and a few freckles around his nose who never wanted the life of a celebrity. Just acceptance and being able to make some small difference under the sky while my head was still hovering above my feet was all I wanted. Music and the platform it offered, was for me, the only way that I knew how to attempt it.

But now, I had gone and done it, and here I was. I thought about that. The question I had posed to Sis over and over, "Do I belong here?" The answer was still elusive, but again, I concluded that I had done everything to screw it up. There had to be a bigger plan and I sure wished it would reveal itself, but for now, it was time to hit the stage.

Stare into the light Wayne, stare into the light.

Chapter 21

Independence United

In the early to mid-two-thousands, mainstream country radio was beginning to catch a new groove, driven much by the discoveries of a younger audience to its ranks. As such, the timing for my sound had been perfect. The top brass of the industry still maintained their role as the gatekeepers and were going to rule musically and morally as they saw fit, even with regard to social declarations. Not only were the country charts all white, but when word leaked out about the sexual preferences of artists like KD Lang, Chely Wright, and Ty Herndon, their songs came off the playlists and fast. Turns out the country audience could be 'funny about that sort of thing.' What's that smell? Sorry, I think a little more bullsh*t just jumped off the page. The powers-that-be should have spent some time on the bus with me. Those dudes behind their music row desks didn't know crap about music or its audience, who, in my experience, are embracing of all. Great music was being muted, and that's a shame.

Sis and I only ran into one—just one—radio guy we didn't like. I THINK it was in Minnesota and, I THINK his name was Dave. Not only was he not going to play my record no matter how high it made it on the charts, but, he would never play _any_ independent artist. Well, now that's catering to the listeners of your station, buddy. I didn't care if he didn't like my record or if he didn't like me, but I cared a hell of a lot about the format that had helped to mold me growing up. I cared even more for the plight of independent artists who didn't want to be controlled by these types of assholes. His six-feet-something tall of arrogance really pissed off my five foot seven of twang I'll tell ya that right here in black and white. Yupp... but I told *him* that right there in color. Bottom line, we won't be sending the next WW single to ... I THINK Dave in ... I THINK Minnesota, BUT, for those of you in and around Duluth, keep an ear out for ole WW. Ya never know ah?

Our fan base grew bigger, as did the concerts and the venues. The people, as always, were rejuvenating to our tired souls, and the radio stations were leading the way. They gave us label advice. They gave us calm in the storm, they gave us encouragement, and they gave us guidance. Most of them didn't care for the structure of the business any more than we did, and they quietly loved it when someone would rise against the status quo.

I wasn't the only one combating the status quo. In late October 2006, Sis and I began to talk about uniting the forces for independence. Soon, there was a huge writing ensemble going on at our suite in Nashville. What another 'wow' moment that night was. The agenda was to write a song with a positive message that a group of well-known indie artists would record together. Sis filled the room with snacks and soda and the hit writers, artists, and friends soon filled the chairs. Mark Collie had penned several hits that he had recorded, as well as many that other artists have taken to the charts. When Mark entered the room, it changed. The whole atmosphere became swollen with an air of intense and unique skillfulness. He is an artist who is multi deep, but the kind of deep that makes everyone around him want to wade into like a pool on a summer's day. It was this magnetism that took him to the radio airwaves and onto the big screens as well. He co-starred with Steven Seagal in *Fire Down Below* and with John Travolta in *The Punisher*. He is also known for his many appearances on *Walker, Texas Ranger* and the *Nashville* series. Mark had publicly fought his battles but remained in the ring and hit back hard. Songwriter Jimmy Stewart took a seat. He had become a good friend and had written a hit for Toby Keith, *A little Less Talk and A Lot More Action*. Mila Mason joined us and brought along multi-talented Jason Grainger. Mila had become as famous for her beauty as she had for her chart-toppers *Dark Horse* and *That's Enough of That*. Jimmy Fortune brought his fantastic sense of humor outmatched only by his ability to craft a song. I was not alone in my certainty that his membership in the Statler Brothers was key to the sustainment of their career. He had penned their comeback hit *Elizabeth,* which helped to revitalize the career of the legendary group. Jimmy grabbed my guitar and led us all in a sing-along of one of their greatest songs, *Counting Flowers on The Wall,* before we got down to business. We all broke the standard rules and ate too much junk food. Combined, the talent in the room knew how to fill a blank page, and after a lot of fun, a song was born.

The video for *Dare the World* was filmed live during the recording process of the sessions. The singers on the record were all former major label artists who combined, had made millions for the logo vendors that had been attached to their names when they were the 'flavor of the day.'

Former country sex-symbol, Bryan White, kicked off the songs' opening lyrics *Crank up the bass, turn up the tweeters.* Bryan had ridden the top of the charts with songs like *Rebecca Lynn, Someone Else's Star,* and had a hit duet with Shania with *From This Moment.* John Berry joined us in the studio and brought his vocal wonders to the mic. John also knew the feeling of having hit records with *Your Love Amazes Me* and *Kiss Me in The Car.* Linda Davis showed up wearing her ever-present and loving personality like a bright sweater. Anyone in Nashville would scramble for the honor of having her voice and her harmonies on a record and she had given that privilege to many including Kenny Rogers and scored a massive hit with Reba called *Does He Love You.* Linda is also the proud mom of Lady Antebellum's Hillary Scott. My friend, Kevin Sharp, came with his professionalism and his comic relief, both of which were captured on tape and film. Kevin's chart-topper, *Nobody Knows,* had always been a personal favorite of mine, and having him on the session turned out to be an even greater gift as he sadly passed away not long after the recording, and I miss him. Joined by the writers, Jimmy Fortune, Mark Collie, Mila Mason, and Jason Grainger, the song vaulted to life. Once again, wearing the production hat for a project of this magnitude was an honor of staggering stature.

A small concern for me was that like the *God Bless the Children* project, due to the scheduling conflicts of the many artists involved, the recording and the filming for the video were to take place on two different dates, weeks apart. During that time, we would return to the road. Over the two to three-week span between the filming and recording, my level of discomfort for the WW package as a whole, had reached a new summit. So much so, that I lost almost twenty pounds. This would be a problem for the video that was to appear seamless, and we were concerned about the variance in the scenes. This time, a Nashville friend and image consultant came to the rescue with a black velvet jacket that was a size too big which helped. The rest could be resolved with many of my shots finding themselves on the editing room floor.

The video, however, did in fact depict the actual studio enthusiasm and the excitement of the recording experience, at least as I've always encountered it. The song was to serve as a message to all the independent artists, independent thinkers, or to all who swim against the flow. The lyrics encouraged them to believe in themselves to the fullest degree, combat the negatives, and take the dream as far as they desired, as all the artists involved had proven could be done.

One of the other many perks of being an independent artist is that creatively, at least, you can do what you want to do, when you want to do it. Or, at least what you have access to, and most importantly, you can do so void of the lengthy round-table committee discussions.

This reward was especially gratifying for me and another ex-major label artist on a project that will always be another high point of my career.

Going for long periods of time without writing would always make me feel in poverty of spirit. Like a pen without ink, I felt like I wasn't doing as I was partially designed to do. I liked the challenge and the excitement when I had the feeling that I was on to something worth striving for. The juices would flow when a melody would come to my head that I just couldn't let go of. If I went too long devoid of inspiration, I would search for it, usually from the old cassette player or from notes that I had put down in my 'hook book.'

One day, while on such a quest for stimulus, the title *Something Going On* jumped out at me. I had written it down long ago and had glanced at it many times, but on this day, for the first time, I thought of it as a duet. I seldom wrote songs with partners in mind, but the lyrics began to jump onto the page. The words took on a fun and theatrical back and forth banter that invited an up-tempo feel: "I saw you there, I noticed you, you looked like my dreams come true." The song came together quickly and after recording a quick demo, I began to think about a duet partner for the final recording.

Being a Nashville-based singer, I did a checklist of female artists that I knew, or had been a fan of, and there were many, but while drinking my morning coffee with the radio cranking, and mentally going through the names, I heard that famous song that we all know so well. That dark piano intro followed by an unforgettable, extraordinary voice filling the room with one of the most well-known vocal performances of my lifetime. The song did as a masterpiece is meant to do, it kept me in the present, and it took me back in time all at once:

"Turn around, every now and then I get a little bit lonely and your never com'n round, Turn around, Every now and then I get a little bit tired of listening to sound of my tears."

I had been a fan of Bonnie Tyler's since the day I heard the first note of *It's A Heartache*. Her records had always been ahead of their time and to me, the quality and freshness of her music never faded. She had the uniqueness about her that made her a true artist. From *Total Eclipse of the Heart* to Kevin Bacon shaking his ass in time to her rocking smash *I Need A Hero* in the movie *Footloose*, Bonnie had become a pop icon. I knew by the third sip of coffee who I wanted for my duet partner.

Her manager, Matt Davis, was not only excited about the idea, but a fast mover as well. By the end of the day, he had delivered the demo of *Something Going On* to Bonnie and she loved it. The song had now been born from a one-line title that had been laying around in my hook book, into a new life of planning stages for studio dates with one of the industry's most famed performing icons.

Wow! Things have changed since my first recording session back at Hilltop Recording Studios so many years ago. With Pro Tools studio technology, I produced the studio musicians for the song in Nashville, and then added my vocals to the record in my Vermont home studio. When I finally got Bonnie's vocal tracks delivered via WAV files to be added to the final track, I was amazed. Her pop rock and unique husky delivery blended perfectly with my country design and the combo and the production was monumental to me as an artist, as a writer, and as a producer.

Not long after the record was done, Sis and I met Matt, Bonnie, and her husband, Robert in New York City; Bonnie and I talked music and she and Sis talked shopping and clothes. She is as cool as she sounds. Back in my home studio, I went out and blasted the duet before I headed out for my nightly walk. Passing the old school site was surreal under that moonlit sky. That little freckled faced boy who had hidden in the corners of the playground, had just rattled the speakers of a new duet with a renowned pop icon – go figure.

Chapter 22

Songs in Time

"There's a story from the past
With four girls gone by misguided hands
And everybody heard the blast
In 63 in Birmingham."

— *PAINTED HANDS,* WAYNE WARNER

It's strange, isn't it? How music notes have been such life partners to us. Even before we could comprehend words, melodies would be used to lure us to sleep at our infancy. At the other and far end of the spectrum, as I sadly watched my grandfather's bright and generous mind become dim and completely stolen of everything past and present by Alzheimer's disease, a simple harmonica would lure him back to a time, and in time and tempo with us, if only for a song. A song can also introduce us to seasons, places, and events we never dreamed of.

It was also at this time, that I began the production process on a song that I was passionate about. This would be the completion of a song idea that dug into my soul back when we were rolling down the highway many years before.

I'm not sure why the bus had stopped, if it was re-fueling or re-stocking. From my room at the back, I could tell that the band members were jumping on and off to run into whatever store or quick-fix we were at. As soon as we were back in motion, I answered a tap at my door to find Scott. He handed me a *Time* Magazine that he had picked up for me with good ole Johnny Cash on the cover.

Scanning through the pages, a photo and a story captured my attention. Maybe it was the old, grainy picture, maybe it was the way the headline was phrased, or perhaps it was because I was missing my own boys that made the photo of this young lad leap into my soul. Whatever it was, the miles passed quickly as I sat on that couch and became fixated on the story called *The Legacy of Virgil Ware*.

Thirteen-year-old Virgil was totally unaware of the historic 16th Street Baptist Church bombing that took place just down the road from where he was that day in Birmingham, Alabama, or that four young girls would lose their lives in that explosion during the civil rights movement. He was excited. Virgil had just scored a job delivering papers and was riding his bike. Small for his age, and a fan of football, Virgil never did hand out any newspapers. The young boy with a love for life and everyone in it became the fifth victim of the day, shot by a couple of boys who passed him by on a motorcycle.

I was captivated by the story. I shared it with everyone on the bus. I knew I wanted Virgil's story to be told, but in a fashion that it could be merged with the issues of the past and the present. Once again, I was motivated. I wasn't burning up the charts, but as an indie artist, the radio play and exposure we were getting was becoming significant. As such, I felt compelled to do more – significantly. It was the only way I could remain driven. Virgil was my new source of energy.

The song had to be right. I had never approached writing lyrics such as this. It had to have the historical info, be factual, and have a hook. Most importantly, I wanted it to pay tribute to an innocent child, and I hoped that the 'universal language' would help, at least to be a melodical strand of thread to help weave together the many great fabrics of our human quilt. The song would be weighty, and it took on a personal meaning to me. It wouldn't be written easily, and I knew it was one that could not be forced.

That didn't stop me from cultivating. Every moment that was available on that tour was consumed with writing the right lyric. I did jot down a few notes in the ever ready hook book, but the magic was indefinable.

It wasn't until much later at my home, while waiting for my coffee to re-heat in the microwave, that the melody and the lyrics to *Painted Hands* came so quickly I could barely write fast enough. I truly feel like Virgil's name should be added as a co-writer to the song as it was simply delivered to my pen:

"Black or white, yellow red or brown, come on all, you fellow man. Let's all join, the world around, and hold each other's, hold each other's Painted Hands."

I had tried to make it complicated, yet it turned out to be in such a simple form, a modest melody that just told the story. As such, the production would demand the same approach. With one exception: it too, could have a statement.

I began to record the straightforward basic tracks in my home studio. I wanted the Nashville production to be in the service of the song. I also wanted to plant a seed and a message in the production itself, something that would bring amplification to a universal concern, beyond the song. I set out to assemble a United States choir. The goal was to bring in a singer from each of our fifty states to carry the significance of unity, in harmony and in time. A reflection of hope, and of love for a little boy named Virgil and a cause that we, united in song, believed in. I also however, aspired to celebrate independent artists and individuality. Gathering this ensemble of astonishing and gifted souls was time-consuming beyond belief, and worth every second.

There was one guy that I targeted to represent the state of California. Reflected in his life was much of what the heart and soul of this song and project was about. While challenges attempted to hold him down, he would become famous for the grace with which he could cut the sky.

I'm not one to watch a lot of movies, or television for that matter. I guess I always just felt that it would be more important to create and live my own life, rather than to spend my days watching a fictional version of someone else's. Somewhere however, I saw a re-run of the movie *Breaking the Surface*, the story of famed Olympic diver Greg Louganis. Adopted, bi-racial, and bullied, his life reflected much of what this production was addressing.

Although not a singer, the super diver became a part of the record, and yet another great performer that I have been blessed to know and to sing with.

As sports fans, the boys were excited to meet Greg when he invited us to meet him in Boston for a diving event. With the three of us and our luggage piled into my Mini Cooper, we headed down the road. It was on that trip that I wrote the title song for what would become a new album.

The lyrics and the melody for the song, *All in Fun* came quickly. While the boys were set up for their video games in the hotel room, I decided to go for a short walk on the Boston outskirts. My sons and I were having a great time on the trek and looking forward to meeting with Greg the next day. As such, the mood was set for an up-tempo feel-good melody. I knew that it would be a great title for the new album to remind me to do just that—keep it fun. I had accomplished what I had set out to do and now it was going to be about the music, about living life, and about keeping it all fun.

The song, *Painted Hands* landed on the *All in Fun* album, and I was amazed with the simplicity of the song's structure while combined with such an extremely complex narrative. With its United States Choir, the song serves as another tribute to the amazing potency of music and just like a little ole mouth organ could bring my Grampa back to us for a while, maybe a song could help a little thirteen-year-old boy live on in some small way, and perhaps, even say some things that only he could say.

Chapter 23

Just Between Me and You

For all of us, there are some todays when we just miss the yester-ones, you know what I mean? When I look back on those times now, the highlights were spending time one-on-one with the guys and gals at those radio stations, getting to know and work with fellow artists, and meeting people from the crowds. Not long ago, John 'Bo Duke' Schneider and I were doing an interview together about a song of mine he recorded called *The Spirit of Christmas*. During the interview, he talked about how much he enjoyed his music career in a different aspect to his acting profession because when singing to his audience there were those moments when you were 'one with them.'

There were times when during a performance, I would stare into the light and know the magic was happening, that we were connecting. There were those moments when the song I was singing would take me back to the inspiration of its origin. For a beat or two, the echoes in my head would grow quiet. Even they would be mesmerized by where we had come. It was the kinda high no drug or alcohol could deliver, but yeah, there were moments. During those sweet measures of a song, it was how it was supposed to be. Those are the times that every artist lives for, but I wanted also to know how to connect with the crowd as Wayne Warner among them, no longer just as WW in front of them. I was getting tired of playing the role.

I suppose for those of us who are fortunate to have lived long enough, there comes a day of discovering a new reality. A time when the truth becomes clear that a line has been crossed, one that declares that we now have more past, than future. Such a comprehension can cause a squeaky trip up the steps into the belfries of our minds for some internal contemplation.

I knew that there were elements of WW that had been a fabrication of course, as is the nature of show business, from his age, to his persona and sometimes his personality. With that development beginning on the playgrounds of school, Wayne Warner had unknowingly been setting myself up for judgement all my life. I guess in some ways we all do. I had completed all I had subconsciously set out to achieve, which was of course what we all desire—acceptance.

But there had to be a place on stage for WW the persona, and Wayne Warner the man, AND to keep the WW brand in existence. For me, the guy in the middle, this had to happen in order to sustain. For too long, I had ping-ponged both roles and didn't have a solid grip on either. They both agreed they loved being a dad over and above anything the world had ever offered. They concurred that they needed to be creative and to record music that had something to say and that they had to stay true to independence and help pave the way for those who wanted the same. They differed greatly on how to do so. WW COULD force himself to stare into the light. He *did* love the chaos, the connection with the crowds, the excitement, and sometimes the insanity of it all. Wayne Warner wanted to go home. He would like to get into his sweats, the ones with the holes in them, watch cartoons with his boys, go to every single one of their games, record his music, and somehow make it work while being the recluse he was now being reported to be. On these two dramatically different approaches, the battle would ensue. Both, by design, truly loved and wanted to please everybody. Additionally, a conclusion was reached as to who the two personas jointly equalling 'I' was *not*.

As a writer and a singer, while proudly rooted in the country music I was raised on, I was not pop, rock, rap, country, or any other genre in existence, but instead, one who paints by note whatever is presented by the giver of the gift, to the canvas. I am neither Democrat nor Republican, but an American raised on common sense. My race is not black, white, red or brown, but human. I am neither gay, straight, bi, hetero, homo, or whatever other subtitles they throw out with regard to whatever makes your thighs quiver. If, that's IF, I ever fall in love again, it won't be with a gender, it will be with a human being. When it comes to gender and intimacy, neither WW nor Wayne Warner trusts either one at a range closer than two feet. I am not liberal nor am I conservative. I am not religious, but sure as hell don't want to live without my faith in God.

The DVD of Emmylou Harris was playing on my flat screen again right there in the back of my bus. I remember laughing out loud after I had that conversation with me. Then, I looked in the mirror and said. "Now, will both of you get one ass in a pair of jeans, you have a show to do." Crazy or what?

That show was in Louisville, Kentucky. As soon as I hit the stage, I knew that the one-on-one talk with one had done nothing to aid in calling a truce regarding the disguised contentions behind the mic. I don't recall the reason, but there were a couple of Music Row guys who had come up from Nashville to 'scope' me out. I really didn't know why, but it did throw off my pre-show routine. However, I knew as soon as I strapped my guitar on that something else was different that night, something I just couldn't nail down.

About mid-show, I did something I had never done. My dad had never performed at a venue such as this and I sat on a stool and invited him onto the stage. The band stepped out and the audience was still as my Dad and I took them all on a melodic trip back to Buzzy's Barn Dance. I sang the old standard *Lonely Street*. "I'm looking for that lonely street, I've got a sad sad tale to tell, I need a place to go and weep, where's this place called Lonely Street."

You could have heard a strand of hair hit the floor when my dad so gracefully played that mandolin on the solo. I felt every note and the song did what great music is meant to do; it carried me away. I stared into the light. I wanted home, I wanted my sons, I wanted familiarity. The notes played and somewhere that night, during that song between the rhythm and the beat, I became soaked in reality. Dripping wet with a new fear of the realization that there was a void as long as that Missisquoi River between my new life and my old, and I was drowning in it. I swam upstream. I had accomplished what I set out to do and more. I had nothing left to prove. All the miles, all the meet and greets, all the songs and now, while on stage in Louisville, Kentucky, I got it. I had gone against the flow. I swam up stream. And I am in over my head.

Stare into the light Wayne, stare into the light.

Chapter 24

A Final Duet

"Un-break my broken Heart, un-break my world apart
And make me un-lonesome
Un-tear my dreams in two make me un-be without you
And make it all un-wrong
Un-cry the tears I've cried and make the words goodbye unspoken
Your love is all I need- un-be away from me
Baby be un-gone
Cause you can love me whole
You can make me – unbroken."

— *UNBROKEN*, WAYNE WARNER

I don't remember the venue, but it was in Pennsylvania. After the band loaded in, Sis walked me from the bus to sound check. Right away, I was uneasy. Was it that we had put on a few too many hundred miles on this run? Was it pure exhaustion? Was it a phase of my sobriety, or just the ride; the ups, the downs, and the magnitude in the directions of each?

My anxiety level and insecurities were in unison and their choir was at full volume. Was it one of the faces that had circled the bus as we entered? I had gotten used to the looks, the winks, and the c'mons from females and males alike. Such was a part of the gig, in fact, part of the job. But tonight, while I could see that Sis, Unc, and the band were talking to me, the inner voices were all I heard. I did say hello and shook hands with radio sponsors and venue personnel. It was to be a good night and the show always goes on. But something or someone was off—me.

The place was a bit smaller than I had grown accustomed to, and in my state of mind, right or wrong, I was feeling squeezed and sensing the pressure. I stood at my mark and wanted to run. In my mind, I was convinced that the stage, while roped off, was too close to the crowd. How will this work? Even for a sound check in an empty room. I said, "Where's my spotlight? Just turn it on."

Stare into the light Wayne, stare into the light.

Scott, Unc and the band knew that sound checks were the only time that Wayne the artist, would get short tempered. Time was always restrained and for me, it had to be right, or it wouldn't be. I had heard that ticket sales resulted in a full house that night, but the voices in my head, *The stage is too close, pull the mic back. Sis, how's it sounding out there? Can I get less vocs in my ears? Unc, how's it for you? Can we go over that tag one more time? The stage is too close, I can't feel that fu**ing kick, Unc, will you be sure my guitar is tuned—*

Scott got me wired up for the sound system and the show was on. But they were too close; the voices – the lie and the lies, they're too close, the cameras, the cell phone videos. Stare into the light. Sing the song. I was exhausted. Get through the show, Wayne.

Somewhere down deep, the on the surface-kind of deep, I knew, on that night, that it was almost over. They love me, they hate me. They wanted my autograph, they wanted to throw stones. Sis, when are we going home? They want to throw me out, they wanna grab my crotch. Where's security? Stare into the light. What's the next line?

Stare into the light, sing, stare into the light.

The crowd went nuts as the band kicked off *Turbo Twang* and I could feel the kick beat under my feet. One more song. I always closed the show with our version of Johnny Cash's *Ring of Fire* and the drummer counted it down. I knew the bus was right by the door and I was ready to board.

I knew the song by heart, the band was nailing it, the kick was slammin' and the crowd was singing. I was there, but also somewhere else. I looked for Sis near the stage but didn't see her. I looked over at Unc and the familiarity I had known for so long. I looked for something to bring me back into the moment. And then, it happened. There, just between Unc and I, "I fell in, to a burning ring of fire." My mind saw him so clearly, "I went down, down, down, but the flames went higher."

A boy around eight-years-old, I could see him so clearly. He had messy hair and a few freckles around his nose. He was strumming a small wooden guitar for all he was worth. He was already quite the performer and in him, I saw the signs of what he would later develop that would take him around the country and into a world that, as yet, he could never dream. We sang it together and while the crowd watched me, I was lost in him. He looked at me with hurt and scared eyes, but he smiled, and I knew that he was hiding another rough week at school and seeking safety in a song. He would stare into the light. We had been separated by so much, I had spent years pushing him and his mournful voice of the past away. I had shut him out with song, with booze, and with thousands of miles. I had been discarding him for years. "And it burns, burns, burns." I needed to embrace the hurt and scared child that he was, and he needed the man he grew up to be. "A ring of fire, a ring of fire."

But, right there, through the magic of a song, the hands of the clock were able to reach across the spectrum and bring that yesterday and that now together to play in the perfect time of a song. "A ring of fire, a ring of fire."

What the audience was unknowingly participating in that night was not the burning flame of a rising star going crazy, but instead, they were hearing the sweet duet of a single voice going sane.

The song ended. In the distance, I heard Scott say, "Wayne Warner, everybody. Thanks for coming." They played the outro as I made my exit stage left, but this time, on that night, as the lights were cooling down, something was about to happen that I hadn't experienced since I was a kid. The crowd was on their feet and not a single soul saw it, but for the first time in my career, right there as the curtain closed, Wayne Warner exited the stage – alone.

We had one more venue on the run back in my home state. Two shows back to back and both packed. We rocked through the show and 'Turbo Twanged' the crowd. I listened to and watched the band closely that night. I knew it was over. While the guys were rocking the beat, only Sis, Unc, and I knew that the bus and the band would be heading back to the Nashville base without the singer. It was time to go home. ETA: 15 minutes.

Chapter 25

Crackers and Ginger Ale

"Ohhhhhhh I wanna hold you in my arms again
Ohhhhh living wishing every now was then
To try to stop the tears - pretend it never happened at all
Is like trying to push the river
Trying to climb a waterfall."

— *Waterfall*, Wayne Warner

These days, much has changed as frequency waves bounce around the hills and valleys of the musical landscape. In many ways, you are now your own music program director. You can take on the mission of creating your soundtrack for the day and discover the new and the unknown, play those golden oldies, the top 40 of the day, or a combination of all. You can decide what you love, or what, in your opinion, just plain sucks.

Some of the young talent we are hearing today *blows my mind*. I am grateful that the introduction of social media offers them a platform for you and me to applaud and support them. It also pisses me off, as it does any true artist and many of those in radio, that some of those surfing on the top of our still-celebrated charts couldn't carry a tune if it was tattooed on both cheeks of their ass without the help of studio wizardry.

My sons and I have fun debates about the power of music. I believe that the influence it encapsulates is often used to assault the innocence of our youth. That, much to the delight of our good ole entertainment industry, our young intellects are pumping negative messages via earbuds directly into their brains at high decibels. My boys have their point, which is that these artists are giving a voice to the diverse emotions that are in existence. We always come to an agreement: they are right, I am 'righter.' I have a feeling that I just might get more feedback regarding this.

I still hear some of the people I used to know and worked with on my radio dial, and I celebrate them and their success to the fullest degree. Others have gone mute, disappeared into the quiet corners of alternate stages in life. I guess as always, I'm somewhere in the middle. I write my songs and spend years making an album, but for me, the records I make these days are 'heart over chart' and they seem to find their audience. I no longer wear $4,000.00 shirts for my album covers but instead, have Sis pick up something in flannel and make a donation to charity.

I read the mail I get regarding WW and people still stomp to *Turbo Twang* around the world. It's rewarding to know, that as you read these words, one of my songs is lighting up a dashboard somewhere. I do know that there are a multitude of reasons why WW should have kept going, but a multitude and three why – I just couldn't do it anymore.

As far as the industry of music goes, Taylor Swift has become one of the most revenue-driving forces there is, influencing the way modern record deals are structured. She has since left Scott Borchetta's Big Machine and has signed a new deal that will aid in reshaping the model of recording contracts for new artists that come after her. To this day, I'm not really sure that she is fully aware of the discussions that took place in the make-up room on the set of the *Turbo Twang* video that so affected her career. To me, it doesn't matter. What does is that a whole generation of young people has someone who embodies so much talent and who was instilled with such a great moral code that they can look up to and emulate, especially in a forum that has a famine of it.

As far as the song that she and I wrote together, it had been lost and forgotten about since the day we filmed the video for *God Bless the Children.* Only recently, while going through some old folders, were the lyrics for *The Middle of The Light,* rediscovered and once more I had to think about where the song had come from.

The Big Machine label group continues to make your ears smile and has introduced you to great music from Florida Georgia Line, Thomas Rhett, Brantley Gilbert, and many more. It has also become an artistic home for artists like Reba and Sugarland.

The major label that had 'issues' regarding the colorful dynamics of my family has gone on to make great changes within its ranks and its practices. They have even helped to lead in the acknowledgement, and the embracement of diversity. This is no small feat and it warrants celebration by the general public, and really, society as a whole.

I remain a low-profile kinda guy, or so they tell me, and when it comes to relationships, I still don't know how to do them; I'm just not good at it. I have been spending the last several years being a single dad and have learned things that WW would never have known. Every day of dadhood is a gift, and I knew it would be a greater reward to raise directed and healthy boys, than to repair lost and broken men. In that respect, it was a team effort and by that I mean they raised me, as much as I raised them.

My sons are my best friends and they, along with my work, fill my world. The first time I dropped Kyle off at college in the fall of 2010, I smiled at him; I was proud and excited for him. But when I drove out, my heart smashed like a crystal bowl. Being a dad was my essence. It had taught me so much. It wasn't about the chart action now, it was about other important things that I had mastered, like a quick stop at Subway after a game could sure make a point guard feel a lot better after his team lost by two points. It was about how saltine crackers and ginger ale, along with a long talk by the bedside of a sick boy home from school, could cure almost any ailment. It was about how a teenager's smile can light up brighter than a December Christmas tree when he gets the news that he passed the driver's test.

When I first became a dad, I held my son's hands and pondered how he would direct them in his life. That son did and does use his hands to guide the young minds of our youth. My youngest son embodies both the gift and the curse of an artist and can create music from the sounds of a traffic jam. They both resonate in the sweetest notes of my life's song and in a frequency that I never stop blasting.

I think everyone's life is a song, don't you? And sometimes the notes given us aren't always pretty. It's all in how we play 'em, I guess. I thank every single soul who has contributed to mine. From the timbres of the schoolyard taunts, to the echoes of the intermissions at the dance hall, you didn't happen to my melody, you happened for it. The song sounds even better blended with life's chords of fear and the pitch of victory – we played on.

Joined by those sweet harmonics of a family band that took on the big boys and scored, I still don't know how we did it. All of this, to the tune of a certain river that flows behind my house. I wouldn't change a single note to any of it.

WW knew much about show biz but would have never known the amazing sights and sounds about the real 'hits' of life. When Keenan left for his college in 2015 I was lost, absolutely stricken with the full emptiness of lonely, but I did learn that a heart still beats even after it's broken into pieces. Lungs pump air and blood continues to flow through your weary veins and so, if my weary heart was going to beat, it needed rhythm. A man is a man the only way he knows how. I began to work more in the studio making the records I wanted to make, and letting them dictate the direction and the timing and try to balance the razor-thin line between commercial and personal success. The rebels in radio are still kind to me and for that, I am grateful.

I no longer ascribe to, or even acknowledge, any of the monikers that are aimed at me. I'm just me, and, as just 'me' closes out this time with you, I thank you for hanging out with me. I hope you find your light and that it shines on you, but most importantly, *in* you.

WW's clothes still hang in the closet. I still hear his tenor on my records and sometimes, I will see an aged reminder of him in my mirror, but, as I type these final words, I'm wearing my favorite sweats; the ones with the holes in them.

Shine on.

References

Sony Producer Says Black Actors Shouldn't Have Lead Roles ...
www.buzzfeednews.com/article/maryanngeorgantopou...
An unnamed producer wrote in an email to Sony chairman Michael Lynton that films with black actors — using Denzel Washington in The Equalizer as an example — don't perform well because the international audiences are "racist," according to documents found in the Sony hack.

Michael Jackson calls Sony Music racist / Singer ... - SFGate
www.sfgate.com/entertainment/article/Michael...
2002-07-08 04:00:00 PDT New York-- Michael Jackson threw down a glove on Saturday in his dispute with Sony Music, calling its treatment of black artists racist. Sony executives termed...

Sony Producer Says Black Actors Shouldn't Have Lead Roles ...
www.buzzfeednews.com/article/maryanngeorgantopou...
An unnamed producer wrote in an email to Sony chairman Michael Lynton that films with black actors — using Denzel Washington in The Equalizer as an example — don't perform well because the international audiences are "racist," according to documents found in the Sony hack.

Sony bosses accused of racism towards Barack Obama in hacked ...
- www.independent.co.uk
  - News
  - People

Sony bosses face racism allegations after the latest email to be published by cyber hackers. While the two previous leaked emails embarrassingly criticise Angelina Jolie and suggest that Michael...

Norah Jones – The Big Interview with Dan Rather

Eric Clapton, The Autobiography, Eric Clapton